To   George

with every good wish

from Tony

HUMANS
—AND THE—
COSMOS

Also by Antony Black

The History of Islamic Political Thought from the Prophet to the Present, 2nd
    edn (Edinburgh University Press and Columbia University Press, 2011)

A World History of Ancient Political Thought (Oxford University Press, 2009).

The West and Islam: Religion and Politics in World History (Oxford University
    Press, 2008).

*Guild and State: European Political Thought from the Twelfth Century the
    Present* (Transaction Publishers, 2002)

Political Thought in Europe 1250-1450 (Cambridge University Press, 1992).

*State, Community and Human Desire: a Group-centred Account of Political
    Values* (Wheatsheaf and St. Martin's Press, 1988).

HUMANS
—AND THE—
COSMOS

Exploration and Mindfulness

ANTONY BLACK

authorHOUSE®

AuthorHouse™ UK Ltd.
1663 Liberty Drive
Bloomington, IN 47403 USA
www.authorhouse.co.uk
Phone: 0800.197.4150

Published by AuthorHouse   07/28/2014

ISBN: 978-1-4969-8322-0 (sc)
ISBN: 978-1-4969-8199-8 (hc)
ISBN: 978-1-4969-8321-3 (e)

To my family and friends

Dao is great,
And heaven,
And earth,
And humans.
Four great things in the world,
Aren't humans one of them?
(Laozi, *Daodejing*, China, 4th century BCE, 11, trans.Edmund Ryden)

Contents

Preface

What kind of a universe do we live in? Where do we fit into the galaxies? Where does sex come in the cosmos? Does God explain it all? Is everything made all right after we die? The coexistence of a fundamentally unknowable physical cosmos with our own strange minds can only increase our sense of wonder at the complexity and beauty of the world we live in. This book locates us in a cosmic story.

We live in a staggering cosmos which, so far as we know, only we understand--partly, and only we appreciate--enormously (chapters I and III). And yet by our knowledge and our appetites (chapter II) we are at this moment destroying our own habitat (chapter IV). By global warming we are destroying the very conditions that make human life possible. We have to learn to live without destroying our descendants (chapter V). How can we adapt our behaviour to make life sustainable? If we don't, is intelligence self-destructive?

We need to bring together what we know from science, the humanities, experience and self-awareness. At some point each of these has to be seen in the context of the others if we are to make what sense of things we can.

The world revealed by modern science contradicts both religion and common sense, but is a source of great wonder, a subject fit for poetry and love. Recent advances in science, such as relativity and quantum mechanics, show the cosmos as more extraordinary than we thought, and different from what anyone could have imagined.

How does this relate to our self-awareness, to what goes on inside our own heads, to family, friendship, love, communities, states, global disorder? There is so much about ourselves and other people that we do not know. Our life choices are seldom based on certainty.

People's minds interact through language and culture. Every human group, from tribes to "the West", has its own symbolic system, its own understanding of the way things are. Can people from different cultures understand each other? Although we may be the most amazing entities in an amazing cosmos, how can we humans get along together on this crowded planet?

Many people find meaning and comfort in religion. For many, god or gods have been and still are vital to their lives. Religions give individuals a sense of identity. They bring people together. They teach some high moral standards. On the other hand, they sometimes divide people from each other, and sometimes teach people to do things that by any other standard would be immoral.

It looks very unlikely that there is a god or an afterlife. Darwinism has made it all but impossible to believe in a god who is both all-powerful and loving. But does this debunk all religious belief? Astrophysics leaves questions about the nature and origin of our universe unanswered. For some of the deepest religious thinkers, god is unknowable. Even if not strictly true, do religions still have something to say? Can we still see nature in an emotionally meaningful way? What religions have said about god and how to live may still tell us something. It may be a metaphor for things which cannot be expressed in any other way. We can still find poetry in nature and the universe.

Death is a fact of life. But today we are faced with something far worse: mass deaths, possibly extinction, brought about by climate change, which is brought about by human action. We are destroying our own habitat by producing carbon emissions which generate global warming. Unless we take drastic action, global temperatures are set to increase to a point where human life becomes increasingly difficult and perhaps barely possible. We are burning fossil fuels at an accelerating rate; the concentration of CO_2 in the atmosphere has already reached a point which most scientists consider extremely dangerous.

Climate change is the unintended consequence of scientific knowledge and the actions of all human beings everywhere. If the modern global economy continues in its present form, sooner or later the deep ocean methane may be released, as happened some 250 million years ago when 90% of all species went extinct. As resources become more and more depleted, conflicts will spread. Few if any countries will escape the effects of this. In much of central Africa, "(d)esertification and swelling populations outstrip agricultural productivity", with the result that conflicts in countries such as Mali and South Sudan 'continue to displace millions, pushing ever more young men north towards Europe'.[1]

Can we prevent all of this, and if so how? We need to ask how we can avoid--or live with--the disasters of extreme climate change. What can we do to save our children?

How, then, can we lead a good life, a life that will make us, our children and grandchildren happy? How can we relate our hopes to what we know about the world? We need to deepen our instincts for reciprocity, empathy and compassion. We find it relatively easy to respect others in small groups or if we know them personally. Humans have an ability to grasp another person's point of view. But we are just as keen to get all we can for ourselves, and to keep outsiders out.

But we should be able to behave decently to others by our awareness that everyone else thinks and feels as we do; and by our understanding that we are all in the same boat and that we all share the same feelings about love and death. Since everyone's behaviour in the long term affects everyone else, especially in the case of climate change, we have to act in ways in which we would be happy for all others to act, and to seek the common good of all human beings. Doing what we know will benefit others makes us feel good about ourselves. There is a connection between acting well and being happy.

To resolve the conflict between altruism and self-interest, we need, in the first place, a state whose laws are enforced by common agreement. But, since states sometimes fight each other, conflict can only be avoided if there is some kind of worldwide agreement, and perhaps a world state. Religions help insofar as they teach respect for all human beings; yet all too often religions divide people into believers (insiders) and non-believers (outsiders). Morality does not depend on religion. Reflection can teach us that we should respect all other persons simply on the ground that we all share the crucial properties of self-awareness and personality. This would enable us to treat all fellow-humans as fellow-citizens, members of a single global community. This requires education. We can be taught to see that nowadays our own survival depends on worldwide co-operation.

People have been thinking about these things since human life began. We can learn how to thrive in harsh circumstances, and develop a sense of oneness with all being, with the help of the philosophy, theology and poetry of both East and West. These suggest ways of confronting a bleak universe and coming to terms with it. We can find satisfaction through art and exploration without deflowering the earth. Through meditation we can develop an inner place of still delight.

Acknowledgements

In such a wide-ranging book, I have obviously gone far beyond any expertise I have. This is especially true of chapter I.

I would like to thank my former colleagues Brian Baxter and Luke O'Sullivan for their helpful comments on an earlier version; John Brush and Roy Partington for their patient encouragement; my son Tommy and his wife Emma for help with chapter V; Rob Duck of the School of the Environment at the University of Dundee for help with chapter IV; Vicky Pope and John Mitchell of the Met Office for pointing me to the International Panel on Cimate Change. None of these bear responsibility for any errors that remain.

I would like to thank my son Chris who by the interest he took and his insistence that I get on with it, encouraged me to think the next generation might be interested; and my grandsons Oisin and Fergus who inspired part of chapter IV.

Prologue

The old man lay sick and dying. His son came and sat on his bed. 'How are you?'

'Tell me a story.'

The boy began to tell the old man a story. Lunch-time came and went. Eventually the old man said, 'That was a nice story'.

'Shall I tell you another one?'

'Yes please'

This was a long story because it was the story of the boy's life. When he finished it was dark. The old man lay there, the young boy sitting beside him.

A nurse came with some medicine. 'Are you two all right?'

'Yes thankyou,' they each replied almost at the same time.

The little boy grew older. Eventually he became very tired. He lay down beside the old man.

'Are you not feeling well?' the old man asked.

'I would feel better if *you* would tell *me* a story', his son said. So the old man began to tell his story.

Nature and Science

Human beings only exist for a split second in the history of the universe but we know more about it than is known by the rest of the universe put together. (Of course, god or gods would know much more.)

And today we know more than ever before about the universe. We know far more about why things happen, about how the universe got going and became like it is now, and how the different species of insects and birds evolved. A solar eclipse was first predicted in 585 BCE; now the Global Positioning System enables people to calculate their exact position anywhere on earth. The pace of discovery is speeding up.

The universe as we now understand it is vaster, more extraordinary, and occasionally more horrifying than people thought it was: it is more, not less, amazing, more unexpected, mind-boggling than the universe our ancestors thought they knew, which was amazing enough. For example. there are 200 billion stars in our galaxy, and 100 billion galaxies in the universe which we can observe; no-one knows how many more lie beyond the range of our observation. To cross the universe you would have to travel approximately 90 billion trillion miles (60 billion light years). There are 100 billion nerve cells inside every human brain, each of which sends and receives signals from hundreds of thousands of others; there are more possible synaptic connections in your brain than there are atoms in the universe. Your brain is most active when you are not 'thinking about' anything. One should not be too surprised that the mind "has mountains, cliffs of fall no man dreamed of" (Gerard Manley Hopkins).

One of the most extraordinary aspects of our universe is that there are things in it-- us-- which can know all this. It is mathematics which has made it possible for the human brain to discern ever deeper and stranger, more unexpected and more unpredictable patterns and causes. But no-one knows whether mathematics is embedded in the scheme of things and so "discovered", or whether our own minds 'invented' it. Why should mathematics provide such a potent key to understanding nature and the cosmos? And this same scientific knowledge has made us capable of destroying ourselves by nuclear weapons or global warming.[2]

The world as understood by modern science turns out to be so different from what everyone thought it was like. When objects are examined by modern techniques such as electro-microscopy, they turn out to be quite different from what our senses and everyday experience tell us. Everything around us, from atoms to galaxies, turns out to be different from what it seems. Scientific facts and theories are often wildly counter-intuitive. Everything we see and touch is made up of tiny atoms. And atoms, it turns out, are made up of even tinier particles, electrons whirring around nuclei of protons and neutrons. The nucleus is to the atom as a grain of sand is to the room you are sitting in. So most of what we see and touch is empty space-- but the electrons are whirring round so fast that it feels solid. Electrons, protons and neutrons are made up of gluons and other, yet tinier particles, some of which have not yet been directly observed. 'Every second of every day, more than 6,000 billion neutrinos[3]... whiz through my body.'

Matter can be converted into energy, and energy into matter, according to Einstein's famous formula, in which it so happens that a crucial factor is the speed of light (300,000 km per second; the fastest anything can travel).

Who would have thought that single-celled organisms could evolve into oaks and elephants; that the rose, the skylark, the horse and we humans are all the result of trial and error, of adaptation, of competitive struggle which wipes out many many more individuals than survive to maturity? Who would have thought that by far the greatest number of species are already extinct? Such is the cosmos we are in.

What finally overwhelms us is the amount that we do not know. And perhaps cannot. While much is known about the history of our universe since the "Big Bang" some 12 billion years ago, astrophysicists cannot say whether our universe will continue to expand for ever, or whether it will collapse back down again to an infinitesimal "singularity"-- the Big Crunch[4]; nor do we know whether there were other universes before ours; whether there will be others after it; or whether there are other universes coexisting alongside ours right now, as some versions of quantum theory suggest. Such other universes may have completely different laws of physics and chemistry.

Most of the matter in the universe eludes our powers of observation altogether ("dark matter"). It is possible that parts of our own universe which we cannot observe may behave in ways radically different from those parts which we can observe.

It is possible that humans may not be able, now or ever, to understand what "things"-- the universe-- are really like, what is "really" going on. ("The universe may not only be stranger than we imagine it; it may be stranger than we can imagine it".)[5] For example, it is impossible to measure *both* the position *and* the speed (or spin) of subatomic particles at one and the same time (you cannot measure a particle's speed without changing its position, and you cannot measure its position without changing its speed). This has been called the "uncertainty" or "indeterminacy" principle. The puzzle over the way particles behave is, as the great physicist Richard Feynman put it, "something that will be with us for ever... this is the way nature really *is*... my physics students don't understand (quantum physics)... That is because I don't understand it. Nobody does".[6]

Even space and time are not absolute. 'What events are happening at the same time depends on how fast you are going'.[7] The speed of a clock depends on where you are and how fast you are moving.[8] Space is distorted, time is stretched, by gravity. Space is curved round a very heavy object, so that, when light from a distant star passes very close to the sun, it is slightly deflected. If two people travelled exactly the same distance in different orbits for what they thought was exactly the same length of time, they would arrive back at very slightly different times. Space and time are part of the frame of reference within which material objects exist, part of the relationship between material objects, just like the familiar three dimensions of width, height and breadth.

Quantum physics and the general theory of relativity are both known to be valid on the very small and the very large scales respectively. But it has so far proved impossible to reconcile them with one another.[9]

But perhaps the most extraordinary things in the cosmos are ourselves. (The Greek poet Sophocles said, "Many things are astounding but none more astounding than humans.") We evolved these impressive brains as a way of improving our survival chances, not least in competition with each other, for mates and other resources. We developed a huge variety of complex social skills (some of which we aren't even aware of; think of the way boys jut their jaws or girls flash their eyes). They enabled us to store knowledge and envisage all kinds of possible future scenarios; to make tools and manage our environment. Our brains are the result of being members of a particular species which evolved facing specific challenges.

Once they'd reached a certain complexity, our brains seem to have taken on a life of their own, like living cells at an earlier stage in the history of life. Surviving in a human context required not only a complexity of skills but generalised problem-solving capacities which could be deployed in an almost endless variety of circumstances, from the primeval rainforest to the modern city and computer culture.

Things did not quite stop there either. We could put our powers of calculation and imagination to work not only on what we needed to know in order to survive and reproduce. We developed the capacity for numbers, for inventing tunes, games and stories. We developed abstract thought: if B follows A in one situation, there is a likelihood that the same will happen in another situation; and if it doesn't, we want to know why. (Babies conduct experiments all the time; it's one of their ways of finding out how the world works).

The enhanced brainpower which arrived as homo sapiens, entered a new stratosphere of knowledge and experiment. Brains created their own inner, invisible universe of thought and imagination. We developed a sense of wonder at the universe: not only curiosity but poetry and religion are innate in every human culture.

So the imagination needed for second-guessing other people's plans and envisaging a range of possible outcomes, took off. We began to feel keenly the need to explain things that were inexplicable, why storms come one day, droughts the next. Such knowledge had significant survival value, yet much of it was beyond our grasp. We also found out lots of things that we didn't need to know.

Not having much clue on some fronts, we used our imagination. For example, because in much of our experience things often happen because people want them to happen, the idea that everything around us was governed by superior powers was perhaps the best, if not the only explanation on offer (the alternative was to say, "I don't know" which wouldn't help, and which we're rather averse to saying anyway). So early religions were not all that stupid.

At the same time, our greater knowledge and self-awareness intensified anxieties about what might happen. It brought with it the clear awareness that we ourselves and each one of those we love will one day die. Our capacity for relationships made the death of a loved one much more painful. And we began to enquire more deeply, to wonder about "how it all started". From this to modern science was not perhaps quite such a leap.

Religious and magical ideas made people feel more secure, by reducing the unpredictable to the vaguely knowable, creating an inner universe we

5

could feel at home in. So they assumed prodigious importance for us. People fought each other about what these forces were: 'religious wars'. There haven't so far been any scientific wars and there probably never will be. That would be too pointless even for human beings.

It may be impossible ever to attain a (scientific) "theory of everything". Some scientists think that the very attempt to do so is misleading as well as arrogant.[10](Indeed, although all science is based on mathematics, not all mathematical problems can be solved by mathematics.[11] And logic has proved that there are things that cannot be proved".)

It could be that at the most fundamental level humans are incapable of understanding the physical cosmos. This could be because we do not have the right mental equipment-- the concepts, the language. After all, human brains were not evolved to do natural science. The ability to understand physics and mathematics bestowed no competitive advantage. However, since the human brain is (apparently) the most complex thing known in the universe, to understand and compete with other humans was to understand something more complex than galaxies or even insects. ("A star is simpler than an insect");[12](and genes make far fewer mistakes when copying than I do when writing on my computer). So if humans are a bit weird, so is the universe (to humans).

Nowadays we are discovering more and more about things that we don't actually need to know, which bring no advantage in our everyday lives. Or at least that's how it often seems at the time; actually, nuclear physics and microbiology have an enormous impact on how we live. They bring advantages (curing disease) and problems (weapons of mass destruction, carbon-hungry energy). So in some cases, human knowledge has become not only unconnected from what we need, but a direct threat to our lives.

The Human Universe

As well as the world we perceive through our senses and know about through science, there is a world within each one of us. We sense this inner universe every bit as acutely as the one outside us. We feel sadness and happiness as keenly as a wound or a good meal. Our mind and feelings exist no less certainly than the particles that make up the universe. But they are obviously different.

Inner Space

Every human being is aware of an inner space. It is a given of our experience, of the world as it is. Human consciousness is part of natural history. A mother nurtures it, not knowing quite what she nurtures.

Humans seem to be the only animals on the planet with self-consciousness. Our minds are not only conscious, but conscious of themselves; we can be the object of our own thought; we can manipulate our own minds.

Self-consciousness is as difficult to understand and explain as anything else in the universe. It came into being along with our enormously expanded brain capacity--in particular the capacity for calculation and imagination--which at the time bestowed evolutionary benefits. The things which we humans do with our brains (music, art, mathemathics and so on) have their own logic.

Inner Space

This inner world exists in every individual of every culture, race and religion. The sense of one's self as something real, about which I can say things and with which I can hold a conversation, seems to be coeval with the human brain itself. It was not invented in ancient Athens or renaissance Florence. With all the dependence of early humans on their close family and comrades, there is no point in the human past, so far as one can tell, when individuals were merged in a group self-consciousness. It is proclaimed on prehistoric funeral monuments.

A strong sense of the individual and his plight comes over in Egyptian writings from the early 2nd millenium BCE, for example 'A dispute over Suicide' speaks as poignantly and directly to us as Augustine's Confessions or a modern autobiography. In this case, the man's life-force assures him that, whether he decides to live or die, it will remain with him, and that after death, 'we shall make a home together'.[13] Long before the twentieth century, people felt a need to strive to rid themselves of the burdens of excessive self-awareness.

This inner space of the self has taken on a life of its own. Probably about 90% of what goes on inside our brains is subconscious ('dark thought', so to speak). This is the source of dreams, religious experiences and divine revelations, poetry and music. Problem-solving, decision-making as well as the worlds of the imagination are largely subconscious. So is falling in love.

Socrates (who kick-started Western philosophy) tells us how 'from childhood I experienced a voice...', something 'divine and spiritual' inside himself (this told him always to question everything).[14] For the poet Emanuel Litvinoff, 'the first words of a poem unexpectedly came to (me)... If I failed to understand how the words came, I knew with extraordinary elation that they were a message from inner space' (he was a teenager working in a glue factory in London in the 1920's).[15] The fact, and the experience, of individual consciousness means of course that human individuals are far more different from one another than individuals of any other species.[16] Each person "exists as a whole world that will never be repeated", so that, when someone dies, "the universe inside a person has ceased to exist... the stars have disappeared from the night sky; the Milky Way has vanished". The features of each world within each one of us are different "from those of every other universe that exists and ever has existed within people, and from the universe that exists eternally outside people", as the Soviet journalist-novelist Vassily Grossmann put it.[17]

Yet all our interesting thoughts and exalted emotions have their counterparts in neural cell activity. This has been demonstrated by the enormous advances recently made by neuroscience towards understanding the physical processes and the places within those segments of the brain in which various mental phenomena occur. It seems increasingly clear that subjective experiences and thoughts arise in conjunction with specific and ascertainable neurological activities in specific and increasingly clearly identified spots within our skulls.

What we experience as meaning, purpose and self-consciousness resides in processes and links between parts of the brain. This bundle of activities seems to be "the essence of what we refer to as 'meaning'".

"There is no single stream of consciousness in which all information is brought together by an executive ego... No single part of the forebrain is the site of conscious experience... consciousness consists of the parallel processing of vast numbers of... coding networks... Consciousness is the virtual world composed by the scenarios" within the brain, and the brain's scenarios "just are".

So there appears to be no central, coordinating part of the brain which can be identified as the seat of personality.[18] Or, as Buddhists have put it, inner consciousness is 'nothing whatsoever yet manifests itself in anything whatsoever' (Tibetan meditation prayer).

And yet this perhaps rather humbling explanation of self-consciousness is linked to a further understanding of the utter uniqueness of every individual human personality. "All brains, genetically identical or otherwise, are almost certainly quite distinct as a result of inherent variation in neural stem cell divisions, cell migration events and neural circuit formation. Such variation is created by the unique, probably often random, cellular and experience-dependent interactions that occur during the development of any given brain".[19] As with the natural world, an explanation which on first hearing sounds banal, turns out to increase our wonder (at least it increases mine).

This does not mean that what goes on inside us can be fully explained by neuroscience. Chemistry is based on physics, biology on chemistry, neuroscience on biology, yet each has its own emergent properties. Self-consciousness has its own logic. This is explored and understood, though hardly explained, by poetry, metaphor, religion. Erotic experience can be mapped by neuro-imaging. But no-one thinks that this captures the meaning of love. In human relationships, a great deal of what we experience as meaningful or desirable is connected with--depends upon--what goes on in other people's brains. I doubt whether this can be captured by neuro-imaging. Probably no other human individual apart from those involved can capture the particular flavours of a relationship.

Friendship and Eros

The inner worlds of adult individuals interact most intensely in friendship and sexual love (eros). These are ralationships which almost every human being instinctively recognises and to some extent understands, though few would claim to understand them fully. And they help us to feel meaning and understanding within the cosmos.

In friendship, two individuals share their most intimate thoughts with one another (as St Augustine put it). Human friendship has qualities peculiar to beings with complex brains, self-consciousness and the kind of unique individual personality which goes with these. People may become friends because they recognise in each other something akin to themselves yet subtly different. Human friendship has no obvious or conscious point or purpose; it is not aimed at individual or mutual interests, but, to put it baldly, something one enjoys merely and sublimely for itself. It goes deep within a person. It is a kind of affection which only self-conscious intelligent beings can develop for each other.

This relationship is at once instinctive and deliberate, emotional and rational. Friends can explore new, unconventional, distasteful ideas without feeling isolated. They share a sense of right and wrong. However long they have been apart, friends always take up where they left off. Friendship takes as many forms as there are individuals.

When one recognises someone as a friend, it is as if you already know that person or have met before, in some other existence perhaps. (This is expressed in the Chinese folk tale known as *The Water Margin*, in which a number of 'heroes' (mostly brigands actually) who are the reincarnation of earlier heroes get together).

If one is not going to meet again in some happy hereafter, it makes it all the more important to meet now. So friendship should perhaps matter more to people who do not think that there is a life after death. There is no worse disaster than losing one's friend.

Eros has been experienced throughout the ages by males and females of every age, culture and class. Primitive art highlights the erotic, reproductive parts of the human body. Longing for the beloved is a dominant theme in early literature in Egypt, China and Greece. The predominant voice in the Book of Songs[20] is a woman lamenting the loss of her beloved, whether through rejection, desertion or enforced absence. Romantic love was no more invented by the troubadours or modern poets than individualism was by the Renaissance. It has existed in every period and every culture we know of, and is surely as old as humanity. Most cultures and many individuals have seen it as central to the meaning of their lives. It is the

11

principal source of our sense of beauty. There is no physical/ mental divide here; nerves and brain, emotion and conviction are one.

Falling in love is one experience which all human beings of all races, ages, cultures and classes understand. Homo sapiens is probably the most erotic of animals. People can fall in love regardless of race, culture or class. A Muslim may fall in love with an atheist and vice versa, in a way both fully comprehend. What we claim to know by reason and the flights of imagination may makes us culture-bound; love and lust bind us together.

Everyone knows at some point in their lives what it is passionately to desire physical and spiritual union with another human being. It is eros we need and eros we have to give. Masturbation is not the same. On eros's behalf, crimes have been committed, whole families wiped out. You are devoured by a look, a posture, as surely as a mouse by a cat: no more yourself, there is no escape. Eros is, as the Greek poet Sophocles put it, 'unconquered in battle', absolute in its demands, god-like; untamed, it overrides self-interest, loyalty, ambition, morality. Pursuing it or resisting it may drive you mad; rejection can lead to suicide or murder.

It cannot be shuffled off into another category; it cannot (generally speaking) be sublimated, or replaced by some other feeling or activity. Living creatures have spent more than 2 billion years learning how to fuck; our cultures have spent a few thousand years trying to ration it, with very mixed success. The myth of Hippolytus, driven insane by refusing to acknowledge his love, is paradigmatic, that of St Antony celibate in the desert, restraining his longings, abnormal. To attain the one you lust after is the height of happiness (so long as it lasts).

Humans love one another for what is most individual about them. Eros focusses on the features and the personality of the individual; the soul is portrayed-- sooner or later-- in the face. This has been the focus of poetry from Dante to Pushkin.

The moment of eros-- when a man ejaculates into the woman he loves, a woman comes in the arms of the man she loves--the subtle interplay of two sets of nerve endings, of touch and speech--is the highest form of pleasure for any human being. Loins enter into a kind of discourse with one another as they exchange vital information in the form of DNA. It is the greatest gift human beings can give to one another.

"Whatever comes, one hour was sunlit and the most high gods

may not make boast of any better thing

than to have watched that hour as it passed."[21]

This is how it was 'meant' to be-- how evolution ensured that intelligent beings would go to the trouble of reproducing themselves. We writhe with desire, only decay beings peace.

This is one area of our lives in which scarcity and competition prevail despite all our advances in comfort, security and technology. It is an area in which we all remain wild. There are few people with whom you are going to find it possible to have a satisfying erotic relationship, and fewer still with whom you are going to be able to have a lasting erotic relationship. There may even, as romantic novels have it, be only one other such person; at least, that is how it often looks in retrospect. If you fail to win that person, or if they die, it would be noble to remain celibate.

We often fail to realise just how high-risk an undertaking being human still is. If you want to enjoy life, you'ld better get used to the fact that what's in front of you may be all you're ever going to get. "My soul, do not strive for eternal life! No, use to the full whatever lies within reach of action".[22]

Shakespeare's comedies are an education in the range of erotic feelings and behaviour: love-at-first-sight, passion, commitment; separation, duplicity, hypocrisy, betrayal; reconciliation, forgiveness, marriage. He unites the insights of erotic poetry and Christian integrity.

And eros can become part of that lifelong bond between two individuals which we call marriage, an institution common to most cultures.[23] It requires, is based upon, the combination of eros with friendship. It was pre-eminently expressed in the Indian myth of Rama and Sita, and the Greek myth of Odysseus and Penelope.

The relationship between Odysseus and Penelope is worth looking at. They had only been married a few weeks when Odysseus was tricked into joining a military expedition against Troy. The famous siege lasted ten years, and he spent another ten years getting home (once, he got so close he could see the smoke rising from his village, only to be blown away again). All that time he was pining for his wife and homeland (despite the embraces of the voluptuous goddess Calypso).

Back home, some thought Odysseus was dead (and many wished him so). Penelope was bombarded with marriage proposals (she would have been a good catch). But she insisted her husband was still alive. She used the famous trick of promising to choose someone as soon as she had finished a tapestry she was working on; every night, she unpicked what she had woven that day.

When Odysseus finally did get home, he disguised himself as a beggar. His old dog recognised him, wagged his tail and died. He staged a competition: whoever could string Odysseus' old bow, could have Penelope. None of the suitors could. The old "beggar" managed it. Penelope still refused to believe it was him. Odysseus asked to be left alone with her for a few moments, "because we have certain things we know between each other". Penelope said he should move the marriage-bed into the corridor and sleep on that. Odysseus replied, "You know that is impossible because I made it myself with an olive-tree as a bedpost". He was into DIY. Then she knows who he was. Odysseus and Penelope made love all night and he told her everything.

Eros depends on death. What does not die does not experience eros. If you were not going to die, you would never have children. You would never see those eyes, helpless yet defiant. What cannot last has sharper beauty. Some may think this a worthwhile bargain.

Culture and Community

As we become self-aware, our inner spaces are already interacting with those of others. An infant's self-awareness is awoken through communication with those close to her. We construct our own worlds out of what is given to us by nature, family and culture. Throughout life, the inner world of the individual is constantly connecting with the inner worlds of other people.

Communication with others makes the brain human. Without language, the mind cannot develop.[24] Communication between persons, between their inner spaces, creates culture. Culture and the human brain evolved together. To understand human behaviour you need to understand both.[25] Everyone is aware of the compromises that have to be made between the demands of biology and those of culture (hence the saying, 'all's fair in love and war'; and in the middle of a brilliant sentence you have to go to the toilet).

If you look around you in any street, you are struck by an extraordinary fact: all these people are intent upon their own agenda: where to buy the cheapest meat, when to phone the girl-friend, how to pay the next mortgage instalment. You all cohabit in the same society of many millions of people with the same range and depth of individual goals and drives as yourself. You all live under the same government and are subject to the same laws. And yet there is no, or very little, evolved blueprint for all of this. Perhaps that is the miracle of culture.

Over time, all societies, whether of Bushmen or business executives, develop their own distinctive *collective* emotional and intellectual worlds with their own language, religion, art, their own sexual, marital and culinary customs. Culture is brains communicating with one another in art, play, technique, hunting, love-making, commerce, home-making. Such etiquette, practices, ethics, manners, tastes create a sphere of their own with a logic and shape of their own.

Some rituals which people perform together in groups may have no practical purpose and may look pointless to an outsider. But they create social bonds as well as perhaps giving the conscious mind a little holiday. All this is part of education.

Culture cannot be explained in terms of human biology alone, nor in terms of individuals acting separately. It has its own structure, generated by the relationships between people. It affects everyone who comes into contact with it.

Cultures are means of understanding and classifying each other and the world around us. They are a way of expressing ourselves. Webs constructed half-consciously, they give meaning to our lives. Once in a culture, the individual can become creative, make his or her own decisions, see what is right or wrong for themselves. Without culture, there is an inner desert. It is their culture and tradition which first indicate to people what they should do with their lives, give human beings what they need above all: structure, meaning, directedness. That is one reason why unemployment is such a curse. On the other hand, one can be corrupted by bad culture-- smoking, junk food, sexual prohibitions or permissions-- just as much as by parental abuse. We tend to fill our inner spaces with junk.

Epics, novels, films have the power to take us into a whole new world, where the story being told seems only a small segment of a whole imagined universe. They describe a recognisable world, a believable world, peopled with its own characters and atmosphere. The atmosphere slips between the words like mist, hovering at the edges of one's vision. People escape into them and learn from them. We may know they're made up but that doesn't prevent them being exciting, horrifying. They work on the imagination. And then the story-teller may say something which makes us think the story may after all be true. History does claim to be true; it recounts what happened as if it were true. The power of both stories and history lies in the fact that they tell us something about what we are, where we are in the scheme of things, how we got to where we are, and what our present rights are (for example, the Hebrew Bible, notably Genesis and Exodus). However fabricated they may be, they give "meaning" to our lives. They constitute a parallel social world-- echoes of reality, but separate from it. This provides an enormous release of tension. They too are part of education.

We experience the parameters of culture as already there for us, a world as ready-made as nature itself, existing alongside--both inside and in-between--human beings. Culture predates by a long way every living member of every group. It comprises for each individual a world already out there, into which we step, just like stepping into the natural outdoors. We are all born simultaneously into the physical universe and into the inner world of our parents and culture. The physical cosmos and our own particular culture are both givens, things we are presented with. Both existed before us and will outlast us. Both have to be explored.

But of course there can be too much direction, too many instructions. Over-cultivation destroys originality. Children are for ever asking 'why?' It seems we start off as budding scientists and philosophers, but too often culture stifles us. Babies and young children are able to "learn about the world like scientists--by detecting statistical patterns and drawing conclusions from them... Four-year-olds are adept at interpreting evidence to learn about cause and effect".[26] (My one-year-old grandson once got hold of a large serving-spoon and tried eating his porridge with it. I took it away, whereupon he howled and howled. His father asked him what he wanted, gave him back the spoon. He tried two mouthfuls and then resorted to the ordinary spoon. I think he wanted to find out whether he could eat with the big spoon, and once he found he couldn't, he was quite happy to eat with the "proper" one. Another successful experiment concluded.) The imprinting of culture can lead to domination of the masses by an elite, or of an elite by the masses.

Just as bacteria created the earth's atmosphere, and just as plants communicate through chemicals wafted on the wind, spiders make webs, and a butterfly's wings are its poetry (as well as its makeup), so humans willy nilly create their own special environments within which to say things to one another. These collective efforts enable us to do things quite beyond what was conceivable or possible for earlier humans. To miss this is to miss something fundumental about the cosmos we live in.

The inner world of the group has been constructed by numberless individuals over countless generations. No-one sat down and designed it, though some have contributed to it more than others. Cultures, like languages, are made up of countless contributions of countless individuals taking millions of decisions. Thus no-one quite perishes. Every conversation leaves an imprint somewhere. Every adult engages in conversation and so leaves his or her voiceprint on human language, and perhaps on human sentiment. ("And some there be who have no memorial; they are buried as if they had never been. But their name lives for evermore", as the Hebrew poem *Ecclesiastes* said.) Every tool we use has evolved through countless prototypes, honed by labours of forgotten individuals. Roads, sewers, bridges have all been constructed out of other people's blood and sweat. We take for granted conveniences our ancestors struggled to produce (and we have the nerve to judge them).

The behaviour patterns formed by cultures seem to vary almost infinitely. Each of us soaks them up. Children, babies even, listen to stories or join in singing. There are tales half-heard as they drift in and out of sleep around the fire, mingled with sounds of the night. The awakening brain reconstructs its own sequences of events, its own atmosphere, in dreams. If you know poetry by heart, you can summon it up at will, or it may come to you without being asked.

Even different generations have their own cultures. Each generation sees itself as the pinnacle of wit and wisdom ("people used to... but now..."). It is humbling to discover how quickly the achievements of one's own generation turn out to be something now done with. "The 60s" are now what "the '30s" were when I was young -- passé and a bit weird. What seemed like a final statement, in art, philosophy and so on, turns out to be just one more step on a road leading--who knows where? There is certainly relativity in what we do.

Cultures, like species, compete and evolve. It is not necessarily the ones we like which win out. In life's race, those who stumble and fall may be nicer than those who win. The physically weak or socially inept may be the best at science, philosophy and art.

It may not even be the cultures that would be most beneficial for the long-term well-being of the human species that necessarily win out. What determines the 'victory' of one culture over another may not be adaptive fitness but power or glamour. The West does not have a sustainable lifestyle, whereas some cultures it supplanted did; modern civilization can maintain a large population but only for a short time. Islam spread partly through military conquest, and today uses the threat of death for apostates to ensure that opposing voices are not heard.

Despite all this, cultures do not construct impermeable walls between people. They are human constructs, and humans can always penetrate cultures other than their own if they try hard enough. Cultural "boundaries" can be permeated, transcended. People from different cultures fall in love, compete in sport, read each other's poetry, collaborate in science. To understand a culture different from one's own is very difficult, but it can be and has been done (as 'world Shakespeare day' demonstrated). We are, as it were, scattered around the circumference of the mental globe, and if we dig deep enough we meet up.

Globalisation

So there has never before been just one view about the nature of the cosmos and how to behave. It is obvious that in the last couple of centuries some aspects of Western culture and some Western values have been taken up in many other parts of the world. In the natural sciences humankind has already become a single society. Modern science is a universal language, in which people from all cultures, races and religions participate. Things are moving fast. Computer technology and the internet enable people to communicate across cultural boundaries as never before. They are producing new kinds of groups in which people feel they belong together without ever having met. Tastes and habits, moral and political ideas travel at the click of a button.

Until recently at least, the market economy was coming to be seen almost everywhere as the best way of raising living standards, by ensuring an unhindered flow of goods, labour and services both within a country and worldwide. Since this depends upon legally enforceable property rights and legally enforceable contracts, these too were coming to be seen not just as western but, potentially at least, global values. Recent upheavals, notably the banking crash which began in the US, have cast doubt on this. It is no longer so obvious that the Western economic and political model was all it was cracked up to be. Even so, many individuals in, for example, China and the Middle East view liberal capitalist democracy as a model to be striven for. Even conservatives in, for example, China and Muslim communities often say they want a different kind of freedom, a different kind of democracy, not that they don't want them at all. Some say their own culture had them all along. How this will play out is far from clear. The Western trajectory of "development" looks perhaps less likely to be imitated than it did a few years ago. Or is humanity, after being divided up for so long into different cultural units, becoming united again (as suggested in the Quran 10.19)?

What do we know about ourselves?

People are not just what they think they are at any given moment. We are the totality of our lives, experiences, observations, from childhood to old age, with all the changes involved.

You might think that we should be able to know our own inner worlds better than we know the world outside us. But, so far as science is concerned, it seems that we know no more, possibly less, about the mental and social world than about the world of nature. There is no science of social behaviour which enables one to predict how people will behave with anything like the precision of physics, chemistry and biology.

How do we decide what to do?

Our massive brains have enabled us to take into account an enormous variety of alternative courses of action, weigh them up, compare their outcomes. In evolutionary terms, humans have been able to alter their behavioural tactics remarkably quickly, even more quickly during recorded history. We started off living in more or less extended families, then tribes, then states, and now international disorder. This of course gives us tremendous scope for making mistakes.

Human behaviour is very flexible, capable of adapting to a great variety of circumstances. This is also, as every human knows, a source of uncertainty and anxiety. We are open-ended, unpredictable; in our relations with our fellow-humans, we have to act on what seems to us very imperfect knowledge. Folk stories and novels tell us about this.

This may tempt us to believe anyone who promises quick-fix solutions to the problem of choice. It has led to disastrous attempts to re-design our inner worlds (e.g. fundamentalist religion) and disastrous social experiments (e.g. Communism). The twentieth century was particularly rich in pseudo-science and pseudo-religion.

We experience uncertainty whenever we have to take decisions in unfamiliar circumstances (for example, moving house, investing our life savings, changing our job, getting married). In all these things, we can only make an approximate judgment, based on what, in light of our present knowledge and experience, just seems best. We have to use our judgement all the time. There are no rules to guide us. So Hamlet had a point after all.

Sometimes the ability to suspend judgement can be as important in making a good decision as it is in pursuing scientific truth. The difference is that in practical life we often *have* to take decisions on insufficient evidence.

It seems we have to live with uncertainty in the things that matter most to us. We may not always know enough about what is inside another person in order to make a decision about how we should act. As Amos Oz pointed out: 'You know so little about people who live under the same roof as you do. You think you know a lot--and it turns out you know nothing at all'.[27]

This is especially the case in matters of the heart. We are led by emotion, imagination, lust. Sometimes these may propel us to act "spontaneously" in a way which is more beneficial to us than if we had acted through calculation. (Remember that most of a brain's activity is subconscious and this has alreay done 90% or so of the work of decision-making for us.) "The unconscious is a place of superfast data processing... and rules of thumb about the world that have been honed by millions of years of evolution".[28] It is a mistake to try to figure everything out from scratch; this only leads to anxiety, which may be a brain's way of saying "leave this alone". This is not to say that everything that comes out of the subconscious is right; it does need vetting.

The Human Sciences

The Human (or social) sciences range from history to economics, from social anthropology to psychology. Their data include archaeological remains, inscriptions, documents, opinion polls, statistical records; as well as the institutional structure and social dynamics of all kinds of groups, from business corporations and states to voluntary and terrorist organisations.

In this way, a reliable picture of particular events, sequences of events, institutions, and even whole societies can sometimes be constructed.

To understand human behaviour, we have first to understand human biology and neuroscience.[29] The failure of most economists to build "irrational" behaviour into their models was partly responsible for their failure to predict the financial crash of 2008; they ignored the tendency of people sometimes to go for a quick buzz, the thrill of risk-taking. Any neuroscientist could have told them about this.[30]

Since one evolutionary purpose of brains is to grasp the realities of social situations in order to enable us to act more effectively, sociology ought to be the most 'natural' science of all but it isn't. There is a huge difference between our ability to handle everyday social situations, and our ability to form systematic explanations of how people in general behave with anything like the precision of physics, chemistry and biology. No social scientist predicted the collapse of the Soviet Union. Yet in the early sixth century BCE, the Greek scientist Thales was able to predict a total eclipse of the sun (and so helped win a battle).

People succeed in business or politics without any knowledge of the social sciences. Few social scientists achieve success in these fields. On the other hand, weapons development and information technology depend on the expertise of sscientists, mathematicians and engineers. This is strange.

Public decision-making is as complex and laborious a challenge to the human mind as any scientific problem. Since those exercising political power can only get experience on the job, mistakes are certain to be made. We should perhaps not be quite so hard on them.

In one field, however, the natural sciences too have come up against a crevass between science and policy: climate change. The natural science is clear enough: the earth is undergoing potentially catastrophic global warming due to greenhouse-gas emissions by humans (see chapter 4). It is also clear what the remedy is and what we--governments, businesses, individuals--should do to achieve the desired goal of reducing our reliance on fossil fuels for industry, transport, heating and so on. But how to *persuade* human beings--whether individuals businesses or governments--to act in this way is quite a different matter. Everyone's long-term interests are consistently ignored. There have been attempts to cast doubt on the science itself, to bend what we *know* to correspond to what we would like to be the case.

The human sciences differ quite dramatically from the natural sciences in their inability to construct universal laws of cause and effect, or to make accurate predictions about what will happen under specific circumstances (especially about how humans are going to behave). We have discovered a good deal about how humans *tend* to behave in certain situations, but this provides us with nothing approaching the certainty of the explanation of the rotation of planets based on Newton's law of gravity. All we have are more or less strong probabilities based on an accumulation of previous observations.

One obstacle to history and social science becoming true sciences is that there can be no repeatable experiments. It would, however, help if social scientists followed scientific method by at least seeking to falsify rather than corroborate their hypotheses.[31] Historians all too often accumulate facts in support of their own interpretation without seeking to disprove it. A particularly egregious example is Anthony Pagden, *Worlds at War: the 2,500-year struggle between East and West,* which simply lists instances of East-West confrontation without considering counter-examples [32] When I was researching the ideology of medieval guilds, I found absolutely no support for the kind of togetherness or group mentality which used to be widely believed to be characteristic of the Middle Ages and which I had expected to find. On the contrary I found consistent and widespread support for the supposedly modern ideas of individual liberty and property rights.[33]

It is of course the intervening factor of the human mind that introduces the element of uncertainty into the human sciences. Human minds always possess the potential of acting differently. These 'fundamental particles' of the social world behave much more unpredictably as electrons.

This failure to recognise the limits of social science has had extraordinarily serious repercussions in practice. The history of the twentieth century would have been very different if people had not relied upon false claims to certainty in the social sciences. Catastrophic consequences followed when people thought they had the same certainty in the social as in the natural sciences. In fact, many peeople treated social science like a religion. They tried to re-construct whole societies according to a design which they believed (or, in some cases, pretended) to be based on sound analysis of empirical data. In its naivete and after-effects, this differs little from those who try to act out the dictates of a divine revelation, such as Christian believers in a soon-to-be-enacted rapturous end of the world, or extreme Islamists who believe god commands acts of mindless violence.

Marx's theory of class conflict leading inevitably to a selfless communist society rested on nothing more than an "inspired" intuition. Natural scientists often have intuitions, but they have to subject them to carefully constructed empirical tests. Marx and his followers were convinced they knew how history worked and where it was going. But they hardly ever tried to test or falsify this theory. The only exception was Leon Trotsky who, in 1939, wrote that if the Western proletariat failed to revolt now, one would have to reconsider the bases of Marx's theory.[34] It thus became, in common parlance, a religion. What passed for theory was an exercise of the imagination. Religious certainty has always tended to lead to persecution; what came out of Marxism was as bad as, probably worse than, anything enacted in the name of religion.

This was even more true of German National Socialism. Here was a classic example of people claiming to base a political and social policy on science, on a true understanding of the way things actually are (contrary to appearances). Jews may look like human beings, but "really" they are not. People saw the world as they wanted to see it, believed what they wanted to believe, and based a whole global strategy on their imagination; instructively, the greatest Nazi propaganda film had the title "the triumph of the will". The results were uniquely terrible.

It was the same with the invasion of Iraq in 2003. Any area specialist could have told Bush and Blair that intervention might easily lead to social breakdown. But they were carried away by their ideology (or perhaps a desire to look good) and ignored the facts on the ground.

Social and economic theories can only be used successfully by people who understand the limits of our knowledge about ourselves and how our societies work, and who are therefore prepared to tread lightly. Karl Popper struggled to make this clear to anyone who would listen in the 1930s.[35]

If no-one understands quantum theory, and if the search for a unified 'theory of everything' in physics remains as elusive as ever, it will surprise us less to find that no-one understands the human brain or the human personality; since these are the most complex entities in the cosmos. We may have even *less* knowledge about the human world than we have about nature and the cosmos. We encounter uncertainty in our personal, social and public lives. In human affairs, we take for granted (unless we are mad) a different version of the uncertainty principle--less well defined, of course, than Heisenberg's, but instinctively known to most people.

Religion and Society

People in all societies believe in some sort of god and some sort of life after death. Humans everywhere and always seem to have had a sense of a sphere of being that is not just physical. This has been the consensus of most human beings always and everywhere, at least until very recently. Judging from archaeological evidence and present-day non-literate societies, religious beliefs are as old as humanity. (They may even predate our species; we have no idea what other animals feel about such things.)

That is not to say that all humans have believed in this way. It is possible that many individuals questioned or rejected these beliefs just as they do now. We should not assume that early humans were any more conformist than we are. There were radical changes in religious ideas even in pre-history. People may not necessarily have believed the official version.

With the development of writing (some 4-5,000 years ago), we find people already asking some penetrating questions, in Egypt for example.[36] The Middle Ages was certainly not an 'age of faith' when religious beliefs went unexamined. But it is fairly likely that more people believed in some kind of god and afterlife in the past than today. In most societies religious disagreement is more open today, and there is probably a wider variety of opinions than ever before. Yet revivals of religious faith are also widespread today.

We know that the truth of religious statements began to be debated openly and systematically in China, India and Greece around 500 BCE.[37]

There is no reason to suppose people were not thinking about these issues long before that. A few, especially in Greece, disputed the very existence of spiritual beings and a life after death. The Chinese for the most part believed in the impersonal force of Heaven (Tian); both the Chinese and the Greeks thought the deceased led a tenuous existence. Science and poetry developed side by side in early Greek and Chinese culture, in the European Renaissance, in the Romantic period,[38] and in the age of Einstein and Picasso.

Contemporary discussion about the existence of god and life after death tends to ignore the extraordinary variety of religious beliefs that humans have held. There have been as many conceptions of what the deity(ies) and life after death are like as there have been human cultures. An afterlife in which the good are eternally rewarded, the bad eternally punished, is very different from reincarnation, in which people have the chance to work off what they have done in previous lives. Buddhists reject the very notion of god. Confucius showed relatively little concern for god and life after death. The Yahweh of the Israelites bore little resemblance to the Zeus of the Greeks; and neither bore much resemblance to the Chinese Heaven, the Indian Brahman, or the deities of prehistoric, ancient and modern 'primitive' societies. Some religions have become extinct, for example those of pre-Columban America and ancient Greece and Rome.

Nowadays, discussion tends to focus on the beliefs of Judaism, Christianity and Islam (the 'Abrahamic' faiths), presumably because these are the most widely held religious beliefs today; but it is often not recognised just how extremely unusual these are. People make general statements about, for example, the effect of the theory of evolution by natural selection on belief in god without taking into account what kind of god we are talking about. It makes all the difference whether god was believed to be benign, or indifferent to human and animal suffering.

Every religion comes in several versions: Orthodox and Reformed Jews, Catholic and Protestant Christians (and there are many varieties of the latter), Sunni and Shi`ite Muslims (also with many varieties of the latter). Even though religions claim (as a rule) to express eternal truths and to be always and everywhere the same, every sect has in actual fact evolved over time. Even people who profess what to outsiders appear to be the same beliefs often differ radically (and sometimes violently) from one another.

Even when the language in which beliefs are expressed, remains the same, what people mean by 'god' and life after death may have changed considerably. To be a Catholic in the Middle Ages meant something different from being a Catholic in the nineteenth century and being a Catholic in Germany may mean something different from being a Catholic in Mexico. What one is expected to believe can depend on one's social and educational status. Liberal versions of Catholicism and Protestantism are widespread in some sections of society but considered outrageous in others. Many Christians today no longer believe in hell. Muslims hold very different views about the legitimacy and methods of armed struggle (jihad).

Again, people vary in their attitudes towards their own beliefs, the grounds on which they hold them, and the reasons which they give for holding them. Some who believe in god and an afterlife are just as willing to discuss these beliefs, are just as open-minded about what may or may not be true as an atheist or agnostic. They are prepared to listen to contrary evidence and argument. Thus, while the content of their beliefs may be 'religious', their method of arriving at them may be philosophical. Within Judaism, Christianity and Islam, some believers interpret their respective scriptures in such a way as to accomodate new ideas, such as evolution, and new moral options, such as contraception. For others of the same faiths such things are abhorrent. The differences between liberals and fundamentalists in any faith is sometimes as great as those between people of different faiths.

Then there are 'secular' religions, such as Communism and Nazism, which reject, or make no reference to, a god or an afterlife. Their adherents believe none the less in certain propositions without questioning and despite contrary evidence. They have revered texts and infallible leaders; for the Nazis, "The new god was the German *Volk*, and Hitler was its prophet", as Hugh Seton-Watson put it. They kill non-believers.

What do Religions do for people?

It is not easy to do without 'god' in human language. We need some expression for the structure of things, the totality of being. We say to children or someone we are not going to see for a long time, 'God bless': an acknowledgement of many unkowns. Religious language may be one of the earliest forms of human speech.[39]

What do religions do for people?   Since they seem to have appeared alongside human intelligence, it seems likely that they served some purpose. What advantages, then, could religions have given humanity?

Religions are a bit like shorthand or perhaps writing itself, mathematics even: that is, a kind of code without which we cannot adequately communicate what we mean (a secular person may say 'god bless you' to his or her child and mean it). To ask whether it is true, whether we 'believe' in it could be irrelevant, a category mistake.

Believing in god or gods seems to make sense of our lives, above all of the fact that we die. It seems to have been a fairly typical experience that nothing else did. This is made starkly clear in 'primitive' religions. Our brains, evolved to deal with the practical issues of survival, social bonding and competition, were at the same time confronted with the unanswerable question of why we are here and the overwhelming sorrow of death. The poets and philosophers of classical Greece (6th to 4th centuries BCE) found conventional religion unsatisfactory and developed new ways of penetrating the mysteries of life but most of them still concluded with some sense of divinity. Aeschylus declared "Zeus, whoever he may be, if that's what he likes to be called, that's what I will call him. I have weighed it all up, and I can't find anything but Zeus if I'm really to throw this pointless burden off my mind".[40] Similarly the Upanishads and the Hebrew prophets based new understandings of the human predicament on their theology.

Most of us develop a sense of ourselves, of where we and the people around us stand in relation to the cosmos. All human beings everywhere have interpreted the world in *some* way. We spend quite a bit of time interpreting our own lives and other people's lives to ourselves and each other. Religions provide a template on which to interpret life's experiences. They act as a lens through which people can think about themselves, other people and the cosmos. They interpret personal experiences for us. They give us a language in which to describe what is otherwise indescribable, and to make some sort of sense of what is otherwise intolerable: the world was made by god, what happens to us is the decree of god (or fate), things will work out all right in the end, we and our loved ones live on after death. We long to rest our fevered minds in some ultimate being. We yearn for a heart in things. Without religion, life easily becomes bleak.

New religions attempt to re-construct our inner world, and often society as a whole, according to a premeditated design devised by an inspired individual: hence 'prophecy', 'revelation'.

It seems to have been through religions that we humans, with our vastly increased self-awareness, were able to cultivate and bring order into our inner worlds. Religions may make great demands on individuals (the slaughter of our best animal, fasting and sexual abstinence); but they provide a sense of purpose, of what we should do with our lives. Sometimes they offer personal communion with god, the ecstasy of mystical experience. Those who feel they are not appreciated, or whose merits go unrecognised, can be comforted by the thought that god sees all and everyone will get their due rewards after death. To lose one's faith can be to lose much of one's hope and sense of self.

The importance of belief in god and life after death to individual human beings is most clear when we are faced with sorrow, disaster or death. Believers have an explanation for what they suffer; they have something to turn to even if their own loved ones are not around. The worst disasters can be seen as part of a greater pattern, with recompense in another life. The deeper your plight, the greater your need for meaning. Niels Bohr, scientist and atheist, once remarked: 'acceptance (of the spiritual content of religion) fills the individual with strength of purpose, helps him overcome doubts and, if he has to suffer, provides him with the kind of solace that only the sense of being sheltered under an all-embracing roof can give'.[41] Even an unbeliever can be moved by religious music.

It is terrible to think that someone close to you has gone for ever. It is terrible to think that we ourselves will one day altogether cease to exist. You want an explanation, and if you can't explain one way, you try another. When someone dies, we can hardly not ask what has happened to them. We can hardly not ask what is going to happen us. So the Indian god-man Krishna: "we all have been for all time... If any man thinks he slays, and if another thinks he is slain, neither knows the ways of truth. The Eternal in man cannot kill; the Eternal in man cannot die".[42]

If far-seeing intelligence improved our chances of survival against the forces of nature, doesn't it also make what we do experience heartbreakingly savage? Doesn't it make the world heartless and mindless? Without religion we might no longer have the will to survive. Most religions reassure people that there is after all justice and benevolence in the cosmos; though some religions are more consoling than others.

Is it possible, then, that the burden of individual self-consciousness which came with human brainpower made the development of religious belief necessary for survival itself, let alone success? Religious ideas, working at a tangent to the world of experience, show us certain possible developments of it, partly to explain it but probably even more to buoy us up, give us courage to confront our difficulties, comfort the afflicted. Whether they are *true* or not is not the point.

All this made a kind of sense; it made our surroundings and prospects bearable for conscious intelligent beings whose age-long experiences and social interactions had developed acute sensibilities to our own and other people's sufferings and death. We humans, with enormous brains (evolved through social interaction) may need religion not only for social stability but also to make some kind of emotional sense of the cosmos, to prevent life's experiences and prospects being bleak, the cosmos inhospitable. Religions bring us intimations of a serener realm.[43] Some recent research suggests that believers are on the whole happier than unbelievers. People brought up in modern secular societies feel an urge to "believe in something". This has to be respected.

The irony of all this is that a religion can only provide these incalculable benefits if we believe it to be true. Once you question it, once you doubt it, it loses its power of reassurance. It would be unwise to build your sense of self on something which might after all not be there. You cannot place your trust in a mere probability.

Religious belief has comforted many; it has given rise to great works of art. But it can also undermine the sense of self, by making people think they have to conform to someone else's norms for example. Mystical experience does not get rid of uncertainty, unhappiness, even unbelief (I know this from experience). Religions have created heroes, benefactors, mystics; but also misfits and terrorists. There is the poet-mystic Rumi and there is al-Qaeda. Christian fundamentalism can be emotional terrorism, spiritual rape. It is difficult to recover: the very means of recovery--self-knowledge--are damaged. Religion can become the junk food of the soul.

The ancient Greeks had a "deepened awareness of human helplessness"; and they were perhaps the least pious and most creative culture ever.[44] Their poets and dramatists did not come up with neat solutions and moral certainties. They look at things from all sides, and leave the audience to make up their own minds. Their gods were often ruthless megalomaniacs. Greek philosophers taught people how to cope with the extremities of being human without the emotional support of religion. Philosophy and science started here. Christian philosophers of the European Middle Ages, on the other hand, while they give both sides of every question, (even "whether god exists?") invariably came down in support of orthodoxy.

Whether religious belief uplifts or debases partly depends on whether it is compatible with what we really think, with the picture of the world we live in presented by our everyday knowledge and science. Religious belief, if it is to inspire people, must not contradict what we know.

Religion and Community

Religion has been an essential part of every known human culture. A shared moral code, beliefs and rituals are the most reliable basis for a sense of belonging. We may call this the religious imperative.

Take for example the Hebrews. Their religion, forged in the Exile in Babylon (587-538 BCE), has enabled them to survive two millenia of persecution and exile. Other displaced nations were scattered and lost theire identity, their language even. Or again, take Christianity: it spread throughout the Roman empire because of its strong community spirit ("see how these Christians love one another", said one observer). Christianity and Islam were the first agents of globalisation, bringing together people of different nationalities in a worldwide web of faith.

Even in the modern West, religion is one of the few remaining bonds of community life. It provides something lacking in modern secular societies.[45] Church congregations are among the last repositories of community spirit. Religious revivals nowadays appeal to the disorientated and socially marginalised and also to people not duped by the promise of wealth or the hope of fame. But, if society needs religion, it maybe needs only a little of it. Jesus told his disciples they were "the salt of the earth"; but you can have too much salt. The one and only true god is like nuclear power, an incredible social force but very dangerous in the wrong hands.

Religion makes for social cohesion by providing a common moral and spiritual language. A shaman, priest or imam can produce a decision which all parties feel able-- and obliged-- to accept. Religion-- it doesn't matter which religion-- stabilizes society by convincing people that ethical behaviour, even self-sacrifice, is in one's own interest; in other words, they internalise norms of good behaviour. In most cultures, god is routinely invoked in contracts and promises, which all human societies depend on.[46]

The result may be to sanctify the existing distribution of wealth and property, social ranks and political authority, as in the Indian caste system. Plato suggested that an elite could justify their authority over the masses by the "noble lie" that they were made out of gold, whereas other people were made out of inferior metals. Social discipline and hierarchy are difficult to maintain without a metaphysic to back them up. On the other hand, a new set of religious beliefs, whether produced by a local prophet or introduced from outside by conquerors or missionaries, tends to create social change.

None of this is to suggest that religions were 'invented' out of malice or deceit, to throw the wool over people's eyes. They were more of a survival strategy. No successful religion was *consciously* invented, as is shown by the vain attempts of the Egyptian pharoah Amenhotep[47], the Mughal emperor Akbar[48] and Stalin.

Does Religion promote Morality?

Karen Armstrong, the prestigious religious apologist, seems to base the "case for God" on the idea that "(r)eligion was not primarily something that people thought but something they did. Its truth was acquired by practical action". One discovers the truth of religious teachings not through 'doctrines' but through 'ritual or ethical action'.[49] Taking part in community life and living in accordance with moral norms has been what religion is mainly "about".

Throughout history (and doubtless pre-history) religions have told people how to behave. They are a source of moral and social rules, usually backed up by some form of heaven and hell. Belief in an afterlife provides an enormous ecouragement for people to sacrifice themselves for others in this life. Rewards for heroism after death make self-sacrifice rational. If there is a life after death to be taken into account, it makes sense to die for others and so be sure of getting to heaven. This gives everyone, high and low, kings, lawyers and peasants, a convincing reason for acting justly. Religious beliefs produce harmony between how people perceive their own self-interest and how they are told to behave. They bring our feelings into alignment with our social obligations. If god sees everything, you are more likely to keep the rules. The police are less busy.

Some theologians argue that morality *only* makes sense if it is grounded in an authorisation beyond human control.[50] One advantage of basing morality on religion was-- and may still be-- that no *individual* is imposing his or her will on society. Coming from a divine source which everyone acknowledges, it has a privileged status. The one who makes the moral rules is the one who created the entire universe. Morality is rooted in the very nature of the cosmos. Similarly, marxists have equated what is right and good with the interests of the working class.

This happens without most people being aware of it; it is much easier because people are not aware of it.[51] If *we* have the power to decide right and wrong, if 'good' and 'bad' are subject to human calculation and revision, we may not stand in awe of them.

Religion was an especially important factor in human societies which had become too large and complex for our evolved instincts to handle, by underpinning (and sometimes creating) new moral rules. Humans need religion not only to help them understand natural phenomena which they could not understand in any other way, but because they-- alone among all animals-- have created large, very complex societies so quickly that there was no time to develop the appropriate forms of behaviour by means of natural selection. We have no genetically-modulated behavioural blueprint for the large societies we live in today. So we have "god".

A shared belief in god provides reasons for accepting one another as comrades in the same society, towards whom we have obligations as much as we have towards our own family and friends. It enables humans to co-operate with relative strangers (provided they share the same religion). In these ways, religion seems to have functioned as a survival strategy in human history. Without religion, we might never have got beyond the extended family.

Many religions (such as Buddhism, Christianity and Islam) have extended the high moral standards expected among kinsfolk to society at large, for example, in the treatment of orphans, the elderly and the ill. They anticipated the welfare state. (Such benefits may, however, be confined to fellow-believers.) Buddhism and Christianity have extended the obligations of kindness, tolerance and forgiveness beyond what is expected in most societies or indeed within most families. They invite people not only to be just but to refrain from retaliation against injustice, to "love your enemies". Even if few live up to this, it may raise people's moral awareness.[52] It has inspired people of all faiths and none, such as Gandhi and *Médecins sans frontieres*.

Some have concluded that, without belief in god and an afterlife, people will have no real incentive for behaving well at all. So is belief in an afterlife, in which good acts are rewarded, bad acts punished, the *only* effective deterrent against wrongdoing and injustice? If so, it makes it very difficult to argue against religion, as the novelist Dostoevsky and the theologian Rowan Williams have pointed out.

The atrocities committed by atheist regimes in the 20th century have done much to confirm the view that we are unlikely to behave well if we do not believe in god, that "without god anything is permitted", as one of Dostoevsky's villains puts it. Marxist Communists identified anyone who opposed them (and many who didn't) as "class enemies" and on these grounds systematically killed millions upon millions. The Marxist philosophy of class produced-- or was used as an excuse for-- mass murder on an almost unprecedented scale, first under Stalin in the Soviet Union, then under Mao in The People's Republic of China, and finally (in case one thought these were random events) in Cambodia.

The Nazi regime committed even greater atrocities, far worse than any that have ever been committed in the name of a god. This has been conveniently ignored by some critics of religion.

But religions bring their own problems. They have seldom dealt satisfactorily with another obstacle to morality derived from human social evolution: the division of people into insiders and outsiders. They have sometimes reinforced this by making belief in the right religion a condition of social acceptance. Most religions make a sharp distinction between believers and unbelievers. A person's status and rights are made to depend on whether that person adheres to the right beliefs and performs the correct practices. Judaism, Christianity and Islam in particular, claiming as they do to be based on a unique revelation from the one and only true god, have consistently preached and encouraged immoral behaviour towards outsiders. Some versions of Islam and orthodox Judaism still do. For them, it is a matter of principle.[53]

Hinduism divides the human race into different castes according to birth and occupation. Those who have the misfortune to be born the lowest have to do the most menial jobs and are treated with contempt. Touching or using the same utensils as them incurs pollution. But they can clean up every one else's shit. Non-Hindus don't even enter the frame.

Believers think they have the one and only absolute truth. Anyone who does not accept this is willfully rejecting what is good and true. The same applies to people following a different version of the same religion ("heretics"). Catholics and Protestants, Sunni and Shi`a, have also treated each other (and in some cases still do) as moral outsiders. One need not--should not--observe the same moral rules when dealing with them; they may be deprived of their property and civil rights, they may be killed.

The Christian New Testament clearly states that those who reject its teaching are condemned to the everlasting agony of hell; unsurprisingly, this has incited Christians to despise and hate outsiders. It can easily lead to persecution. The Qu'ran goes further and states that apostates and, in certain circumstances, unbelievers should be killed (Qu'ran 9.5). In the eyes of many Muslims, atheists and agnostics automatically incur the death penalty. Even today hardly any Muslim-majority state grants equal civic rights to unbelievers. A growing minority of Muslims justify random killing of outsiders. In all religions it is the most fervent believers who seem to be the most intolerant of outsiders. Do such teachings come from the author of the cosmos we know?

Morality can be undermined by the beautiful feeling of religious identity. As well as bringing about social cohesion within its own community, belief in god and life after death produces strife between people of different beliefs. The parties see no reason to compromise. This derives from the nature of religious faith based on revelation: it is "true", and if some people don't get it, they're not just mistaken but radically evil. It is this same attitude which makes "us" radically right ("saved", etc.)

We have seen that religion helps people live together in large states. But this did not bring an end to human conflict. Wars between states can be even deadlier than wars between tribes. They are sometimes seen as conflicts between different races or different faiths. As a rule, religion can only help resolve conflicts between people of the same religious community; in the case of conflict between people of different beliefs, religion exacerbates it.

War between states can best be overcome if everyone considers themselves to belong to a single human society. And the ideal of cosmopolitanism, that all human beings should be treated as members of a single society,[54] came from philosophy rather than religion. Nowadays many religious believers do indeed uphold human rights for everyone regardless of their belief. But recent improvements in the treatment of non-believers have been inspired by moral ideas deriving from secular ways of thinking (notably, Stoicism and the Enlightenment).

Furthermore, religious morality tends to be based on rules. Some of these are uncontroversial, such as 'do not steal', 'do not murder', 'do not commit adultery' and so on. Rules are useful, a kind of quick guide on how to act. But they have to be interpreted and applied to different situations. Moral judgement by individuals in specific situations has to be seen as a normal part of everyday moral practice, as has been recently emphasised in the development of "virtue ethics".[55] By reducing the scope for individual judgement in decision-making, religion can stunt the growth of the virtue of "prudence". (On the other hand, the Christian idea of a 'holy spirit' as a divine gift residing in every individual believer, explicitly justifies interpretation according to circumstances.)

Some religious interpretations can be arbitrary and lead to immoral behaviour. Does 'do not murder' apply to abortion? Does it apply to euthanasia? Does it apply to war? Religions often do not give any clearer answers than secular morality, and they may sometimes gives what to many seem to be the wrong answer (for example, the complete ban on euthanasia).

Sex and marriage tend to loom large in religious moral teaching. Masturbation and sex before marriage are widely forbidden. So too is contraception. Religious people object to contraception because they believe that the sexual act was created by god for the purpose of having children. This was indeed why strong sexual desires evolved. But it is not at all clear why this should mean that contraception should be banned altogether. (Using contraception some of the time doesn't stop people having children!) This looks like a case of a specific rule being deduced from the general rule against adultery and then made equally immutable. Since the introduction of modern medicine, this has led to overpopulation and poverty. It has facilitated the spread of AIDS (not to mention the exhaustion of females). Here the religious mentality seems to run counter to intelligent interpretation.

It is only if one believes that a deity established copulation as part of a master plan that one can deduce that its original ("natural") form must be adhered to in all circumstances, and that to "interfere" with it by preventing conception is "sinful" ("against nature"). What we are up against here is not just a certain type of moral thinking but a religious view of the way humans came into being. Several other species in fact manipulate their sexual activity in some way so as to maximise pleasure. A perfectionist idea of creation does not correspond to what we know about both early humans and other animals. The same goes for the ban on masturbation which, as we know, is widely practised among animals.

Some teachings of some religions are quite clearly immoral, such as the human sacrifices demanded by Inca religion and the random killing of non-believers by Muslim extremists. Then there is the subordination of women to men. In Hinduism and Islam women have sometimes had their genitals mutilated, and been forced into marrying men they neither knew, nor, when they met them, liked. Communism, on the other hand, liberated women and put them on an equal footing.

Some religiously inspired moral rules are trivial, such as not working on the Sabbath (or Sunday) and not eating pork. Such ritual rules tend to be given the same status as moral rules. (In the Ten Commandments, keeping the Sabbath actually precedes the command not to commit murder.) This objection cannot be levelled at Christianity: one of the main points of the teaching of Jesus was that you don't have to keep ritual rules.

On the other hand, sex and marriage are an area in which Christianity has the same kind of specific and detailed absolutist injunctions and prohibitions as Judaism and Islam. Divorce is forbidden in the Catholic and some Protestant traditions. A woman or a man in a deeply unhappy marriage is not allowed to seek divorce under any circumstances. Christian and Muslim teaching on marriage and divorce have recently changed but largely due to pressure, once again, from *secular* philosophy.

One problem with basing morality on religion is that there are several of them, each claiming that its own moral code is the one and only right one. So once people of different faiths come together in the same society, as they do almost everywhere today, there is no way of settling who should do what (other than moral philosophy).

Finally and most crucially, religion can only be the basis of morality if people actually think god and the afterlife actually exist. Once people doubt this, the moral code based on religion loses its force. So to make people behave morally, religions must relate to current perceptions of the way the world works. Otherwise, the promise of heaven and the threat of hell are worth no more than the shares of a company that has gone bust. (The American political philosopher Leo Strauss suggested that the educated leaders of society should encourage belief in religion in others, even if they did not believe in it themselves, in order to prevent social and moral breakdown.) Unless people genuinely believe in the current religion, you are back with anarchy (or moral philosophy) again.

There are, as we will see in chapter V, reasons for moral behaviour which have nothing to do with god or an afterlife. Moral norms *can* be objectively grounded--based on something outside ourselves and outside society--without invoking 'god' or an afterlife. There are clear and convincing reasons for behaving morally based on human self-awareness and practical intelligence, which do not depend on religious belief. There is already within us a standard of moral measurement which is as much "out there" as if it came from "god". Reasons for being moral, based not on divine revelation but on observation, reflection and analysis have been around at least since the time of Confucius and Socrates. These do not depend on who said what.

The problem is: do most people have the time and ability to grasp these reasons? Even if moral behaviour is not logically dependent on religious belief, will *most people* in actual fact behave morally without religious belief? If moral philosophy is to fill the gap left by religion, it has to be something *everyone* can understand. But isn't it just as convincing to say to a child, "How would you like it if someone did that to you?" as to say, "If you do that, you will go to hell"?

Religion and Truth

Does God Exist? Do we Continue to Live after we have Died?

We have seen that all the spiritual and moral advantages that religions have to offer us depend upon their being believed to be true. Religions are statements about reality. They attempt to interpret the cosmos and our place in it, to explain how we got here, why we are like we are, why the world is as it is. They seek to explain why unexpected things happen to us, like diseases, famines, death. Religions usually give an explanation of the origins of the natural world, and the purpose of human life. They explain unusual natural events, such as storms or volcanoes, and the ups and downs of our own lives, as being caused by unseen forces acting with deliberation not unlike human beings.

They tend to say that people continue to have some sort of meaningful existence after death. We mortals should take these powerful beings into account in what we do, try to please them, induce them to behave favourably towards us, by offering them gifts and refraining from inappropriate behaviour which they dislike. These forces--gods--sometimes communicate with select individuals.

The Jews were unusual in conceiving only one god (Yahweh) who was absolutely supreme and all-powerful, that is, responsible for everything. Before that, people believed in a whole society of gods. The Jews denounced all other so-called gods as false, non-existent. All other religions were mere inventions of the human imagination. Nowadays when we speak of 'god' we usually mean it in this Judaic sense.

But does this god--any god--exist? If so, what is 'he' like? Do we continue to exist after we have died? If so, what are we like then? Karen Armstrong is surely wrong to say that you can become convinced of the truth of religious doctrine by living it.[56] (I tried for thirty years and failed.) Taking part in rituals and acting correctly might influence your view of the world as a child, but it is unlikely to change it as an adult. Armstrong uses the valid point that religions have to be taken in their ethical and social context, as a way to avoid answering the question whether religion does or does not tell us the truth about how the world is, to avoid asking whether god exists or not. Without an answer to that question we do not have religion as we know it. It sounds like an invitation to pretend that the truth question does not matter that much.

The idea of a creative deity explains what was otherwise inexplicable: the extraordinary beauty and order of the natural world, of stars, oceans and bodies. Such order and beauty made it reasonable to conclude that these things had been designed by an all-powerful, all-knowing being. Otherwise, one would just have to say, "we don't know".

But the works of nature turn out with depressing frequency to have natural scientific explanations. Recent advances in knowledge repeatedly come into conflict with what we thought we knew about the nature of the universe, about 'how it all started'. They have also come into conflict with how we view ourselves, not least in the theory of evolution by natural selection. The complexity of the heavens is explained by the aftermath of the big bang. The intricate order and subtle interdependence of living organisms is explained by evolution through natural selection.

Does this make these things any less wonderful or beautiful? Some think it makes them more wonderful. But it means that we no longer need the idea of an intelligent creator in order to explain the natural world.

Does Darwinism debunk religion?

The biggest impact of modern science on what people can believe about non-physical things comes from evolution by natural selection. One possible explanation of why the natural world is so beautiful and frightening used to be that it is the work of, and controlled by, an unseen superior intelligent power. The splendour and order both of the stars and of the plant and animal kingdoms seemed to indicate some kind of design, and where there is design it is natural for humans to conclude that there must be a designer. It is natural to draw analogies based on what we know: we humans design things; therefore, surely, the coherence, splendour, balance of the world of living organisms and the whole intricate structure of the universe must have been designed? Such a view long predates monotheism, let alone Christianity.

The theory of evolution by natural selection, on the other hand, has demonstrated beyond reasonable doubt that the world containing living organisms could not have been authored by the kind of all-knowing, all-powerful and all-loving deity taught in the Abrahamic faiths of Judaism, Christianity and Islam (as Richard Dawkins never ceases to remind us).[57] This does not, however, mean that the concept of god as understood, for example, in Hindu and ancient Greek religion is altogether discredited.

The neo-Darwinian theory of evolution by natural selection[58] has indeed demolished the argument from design so far as living organisms are concerned. We now know that all plants and animals have evolved through the interaction of random genetic mutations with the environment. (One of the amazing things about Darwin's theory is that Darwin himself did not know about genes.) The balance and (to our eyes) beauty of any natural habitat with its myriad species all interacting with one another has been brought about by a competitive struggle for survival. Every organism produces many more offspring than can survive, and those which do survive are those which are most fitted to their particular environment. A mutation which bestows a competitive advantage, such as sharper vision, will enable more of those possessing it to survive, and so to pass on the improvement to the next generation. The less well adapted die out. Most animals die before they mature; all animals suffer pain which can be intense and prolonged.

Thus what many, perhaps most (but not all) people used to see as purposeful and beneficent design is now known to be the outcome of a competitive struggle for survival and reproduction in which all living things suffer pain, and most die very young. Darwin realized, and painstakingly proved, that natural phenomena, however attractive to the human eye, like the 'entangled bank' past which he walked every day, were the outcome of evolution by natural selection. Different species of plants and animals coexist, each facilitating the life of the others in their natural "communities". But any intuitive sense that such a harmony has been *designed* is an illusion.

In the biological sphere, there is no master plan, no purpose, no conscious design. The concepts of purpose and design (the so-called teleological argument) have been shown to be meaningless and irrelevant.

This does not rule out the possibility that the cosmos as a whole was created, and/ or is sustained, by a deity. Yet the very processes by which, as we now know, life proceeds and develops seem to rule out the possibility of a *beneficent* deity. We now know that pain and death are built into biology. This surely contradicts the notion of an all-powerful *and* all-loving god. For these are not incidental features of life, they are an essential part of how life functions. The competitive struggle for existence necessarily involves suffering. The injuries and death which animals inflict on one another are inherent in the ongoing processes of biology. Pain is one means of avoiding annihilation; it expresses a desire to go on living; this desire has driven biological evolution.

It is no longer possible to see this ruthlessness of nature as something incidental, tacked on, or perhaps an error introduced at some point after an original creation of a biological system devoid of pain. Pain and death cannot be explained as the work of a malign interferer like Satan in the Bible.

Darwinism (as its author recognized, to his own sadness) has had a significant impact on what one can think about any master-force there might be behind the cosmos. In order for the rainforest to glisten and team with life, for you and me to exist, thousands upon millions of living creatures have been condemned to an early and painful death. This demands a fundamental revision of any notion of a *loving* creator. The well-established theory of natural selection has indeed changed the way any reasonable human being can see the world.

The theory of evolution by natural selection is another example--this time from the realm of life itself--of a counter-intuitive scientific truth. Before Darwin, it was perfectly reasonable to ascribe natural phenomena to a creative genius, a cosmic planner; this was possibly the most reasonable explanation available. But now the tables are turned. What appeared to be "intelligent design" is quite clearly the result of chemical and biochemical events--the numberless interactions of genes and environment over hundreds of millions of years, including random mutations.

Even so, the case against a deity based on neo-Darwinism is not absolutely watertight. Pain can also be a means of learning, and sometimes the only means by which members of a species, including ourselves, can learn. Individuals learn from experience as well as from their parents; species "learn" through adaptations; human societies transmit customs designed for coping. If life had been designed as a learning process, one would have to judge it something of a success.

And evolution by natural selection does *not* of itself rule (
ideas which humans have had about deities. What it does rule out is the
possibility of a benevolent, compassionate deity who is at the same time
all-powerful and who created the cosmos. In other words, it does rule out
the idea of god found in Judaism, Christianity and Islam.[59]

But only someone as ignorant of the diversity of human cultures and
religions as Richard Dawkins could think that natural selection debunks
all forms of religious belief. Dawkins, in *The God Delusion*, hardly refers
to non-Abrahamic religions at all.[60] I find this inexcusable in someone
who claims to be adopting a scientific approach. He does not so much
as mention Hinduism, Taoism or ancient Greek and Roman religion (to
mention a few). In other words, he ignores the religious experience and
ideas of more than half the human species.

Some forms of ancient Indian or Greek religious belief are not
discredited by the theory of evolution by natural selection in the way
that Christianity, Islam and Judaism are because they do not posit an
all-knowing, all-powerful *and all-merciful* deity in the first place. Despite
Darwinism, there could still be a supreme being or beings who is more or
less indifferent to animal and human suffering, perhaps, from our point
of view, beyond good and evil.

As we have seen, different schools of religious belief differ more
profoundly in their views of the deity than most people in the West
today realize. Judaism, Christianity and Islam are far from typical.
(They were themselves products of a long and complex process of *cultural*
evolution.) For pantheists (including the ancient Stoics) "god" was a kind
of personification of nature as a whole ("the system of the cosmos"). Their
god was concerned only with the ultimate well-being of the whole, not of
the parts. The Indian notion of Brahman (world spirit), and the Chinese
notion of Tien (Heaven) are not so obviously invalidated by the theory of
natural selection. Brahman and Tien were not, and are not, necessarily

assumed to be beneficent towards animals and humans, at least not in the same way as the Judaeo-Christo-Islamic deity was thought to be.

Suffering and death can easily be accomodated in some versions of polytheism. The gods of Hindu tradition and ancient Greece could be beneficent towards mortals, but they could also be indifferent or even antagonistic. Ancient philosophers too were not unaware of the role of strife in the natural world: for example, "war is common <to all> and right is strife", said Heracleitus.[61] Plato is largely responsible for our rather dumbed-down view of these early thinkers. The specific function of the Indian deity Shiva is destruction. This idea of arbitrary, violent, terrible gods is much easier to reconcile with some of the observed and experienced facts of our lives, of the animal world, and of the cosmos, than the idea of a deity who is at one and the same time omnipotent *and* compassionate (as Muhammad says in every chapter of the Qu'ran). So too is the Epicurean idea of the gods as remote and indifferent to human suffering and fate.

Thus not all pre-Darwinian believers in god(s) and an afterlife were as credulous as Dawkins and others seem to assume. Even without the theory of natural selection, they had before them plenty of evidence of the harshness of nature, not to mention the cruelty of humans. Homer, in whose poems deities play a prominent role, portrays the bloodiness of battle as vividly as any modern film-maker; and he invariably compares it to the ruthlessness of nature.

Jews, Christians and Muslims commonly explained cruelty in the human and animal worlds as the work of the *devil,* an immaterial being, less powerful than the all-loving deity, perverted, but allowed by god to wreak havoc for a while in the world god had created. This was used (especially in the book of Job) to explain evil in the world, and especially among humans (where it was perhaps most evident).

Today, believers (at least in liberal circles) tend to ignore the role played by the devil in understanding Providence. In the modern West, many religious believers have jettisoned the devil as an archaism, without, it seems, noticing how exposed this left God to the charge of being responsible for suffering and death (he is after all supposed to be omnipotent). Without the devil, it is much more difficult to reconcile the beneficence of god with the observable facts of human and animal life *even without Darwin*, much more so after Darwin. But we can't go back: the idea of the devil is, even to many religious people, a manifest absurdity, even though it may chime with some of our subjective experiences (when we are "tempted" to do evil, for example--where do strange thoughts come from?). The devil was supposed to save god from responsibility for evil. He was convenient, but rather obviously an invention.

In some versions even of the Abrahamic faiths, believers in the goodness of God took this a stage further. They accounted for the harshness of nature by positing an evil being more or less equal in power to god (dualism). Some held that Satan had created the material, God the immaterial, cosmos. (It was, therefore, the duty of believers to escape as quickly as they decently could from the material world.)

Even *orthodox* Christianity had and has an understanding of suffering which could just conceivably reconcile the Darwinian understanding of phenomena with the notion of an ultimately beneficent divine providence. In Jesus' death on the Cross, God is portrayed as himself suffering in the most terrible way (provided you believe in the divinity of Christ). Indeed, *orthodox* Christianity sees god as suffering in and with all living beings in the present phase of cosmic history.[62] The underlying message was that god feels our pain and the pain of all animal creation, as much as any and all of his creatures; and that life--and ultimate salvation in heaven-- are worth the suffering. Why it should have to be so remained of course beyond human understanding. But is this any more counter-intuitive than quantum theory or general relativity?

The traditional explanation of Jesus' suffering and death was that it saved humans from their sins. It seems as if it might just save God from the charge of cruelty. It could offer an insight into the nature of God undreamt of in any other religion. It just might overturn our conventional categories and ways of thinking--which we have seen contain all sorts of illusions about the origins and workings of the material world. Besides, according to original Christianity, most people fail (as in the parable of the sower and the seed, most of which falls by the wayside or is dried up by the sun). Very few make it to heaven, just as in evolution most creatures never reach maturity.

Otherwise, neo-Darwinism has demonstrated that the splendour and order at least of the plant and animal kingdoms came about through evolution by natural selection. It has ruled out the argument from design so far as living beings are concerned. It pretty well rules out belief in a *beneficent* deity. But that is far from the end of the story.

What lies behind it all? What started it all off?

The theory of evolution by natural selection obviously does not address the question of what started it all off, except to say that whatever did start it all off could not have been beneficent or loving as we understand these things. But there might still be a case for some kind of first cause or overall creator and/or sustainer, something outside the existing cosmos which brought it all into being and/or lies behind and above it and/or watches over and controls it. Or something like all this. Remember that, just because it is not benevolent does not mean it has to be (in our terms) malevolent, and it certainly does not rule out superior intelligence.

Physics and astronomy still leave wide open the question of what started it all. Indeed they seem to me leave wide open the question of whether there may not be something more, something out there not accessible to our senses or our sciences. They may even be taken to suggest that there is (or could be), although what that 'something' is remains utterly and in principle unknown.

One view is that our universe began with the "big bang"--"as a *point*... in which all matter and energy (was) squeezed together to unimaginable density and temperature... The whole of the universe violently emerged from a singular cosmic explosion, some 15 or so billion years ago".[63] There are millions of galaxies. The universe is expanding at an accelerating rate; all the stars are getting further and further away from each other.

But we do not know what there was before the big bang, nor what other universes there might have been before ours, nor what other universes may exist at this moment besides our own, or follow it. We do not know why the big bang happened--: "there is no physical way to explain the transition from pre- to post-Big Bang";[64] what happened at the big bang "prevent(s) us from gathering information about events that preceded it".[65]

Some have thought that the universe will go on expanding for ever; that the galaxies and stars will eventually pass out of each other's gravitational orbits and die out in isolation. But the universe is not expanding as fast as the laws of gravity lead us to expect. This slowing-down has been ascribed to "dark matter", which makes up around three-quarters of all the matter in our universe.[66] Recent observations have also led people to suspect the existence of "dark energy" which, it is thought, will lead to our universe eventually contracting back down again to a "Big Crunch".

It is still possible to argue that the big bang suggests an original creator. The physical constants which govern the way everything behaves were established at the time of the big bang; if these had had only minutely different values, the universe would have been completely different; mass and energy would behave in a completely different way. The atoms in our universe would not have been able to bind together in such a way as to produce the molecules which make possible the development of life. "The distinctive details of our universe... seem to be the outcome of what might be called an accident".[67] Our universe just happens to have the particular laws of physics and chemistry which make life as we know it, and therefore consciousness and intelligence--based as these are on a complex arrangement of molecules--possible. No-one knows if some other kind of life might be possible. If these laws had been only very slightly different, there could have been no life, and consequently no human observers of the whole show. This is what is meant by the "anthropic principle".

That the laws of physics and chemistry are as they are, could be due to providence or to chance, or it could be because ours is not the only universe. "The universe may exist in an infinity of incarnations, each one subtly different. Quantum cosmology, in at least one of its variant forms, asserts this to be the case... There are untold billions of parallel universes, all equally real and viable, but with no possibility of any physical communication".[68]

In other words, we may be living in a "multiverse".[69] There may be universes which existed before our own, and/ or universes which will exist after ours, perhaps in a series of big bangs and big crunches. And there may be other universes existing at the same time as ours, independently of it. Such "other universes would be separate domains of space and time". But we do not have direct knowledge, based on observation or experiment, to support such a view. Rees thinks this multiverse theory is the most likely explanation, but it can "be no more than a hunch".[70] According to Greene, "it will be extremely hard, if not impossible, for us ever to know if the multiverse picture is true".[71] Thus, so far as astrophysics is concerned, the argument from design--that the cosmos was created and is overseen by some super-intelligent immaterial entity--may still be just tenable. We simply do not know.

Dreams and Visions

In the past, the many extraordinary ideas that come from people's brains and the many strange things that happen to us in dreams made people believe that they must have come from some source outside ourselves. People saw them as inspirations, 'revelations' by a deity. Recent advances in neuroscience, however, offer straightforward material and scientific explanations for these phenomena, based on the amazing neural circuitry of our brains.

Moreover, almost all the evidence for extra-sensory perception has been discredited. We may experience ourselves as disembodied spirits, or as minds functioning in a non-physical way. But neuroscience has shown time and again that such things have straightforward physical explanations. Phenomena which used to be taken as evidence of a "soul" separate from the body can be explained in other ways. Our individual "personality" is an exceptionally (indeed, so far as we know, uniquely) complex arrangements of atoms. It becomes increasingly difficult to conceive of ourselves as having any non-physical existence.[72]

And we do not need an immaterial soul independent of the body to explain human emotions and thoughts, our states of mind and the way we sometimes feel, our sense of love, beauty and purpose, wonderful and strange ideas, uplifting experiences. Even our sense of communion with the dead, however precious to us, does not mean that those who have died are still alive. The more neuro-scientists understand about the physical workings of our brains, the more they discover physical bases for what used to be seen as spiritual experiences.

Even so, everything in nature and history has a cause or causes. Therefore, it has been argued, the whole sequence of events in the natural and historical worlds must have a cause; there must be an ultimate cause.

Some suggest god caused the big bang. But, as we have seen, astrophysicists are inclined to think that the big bang was not the beginning; it was itself preceded, and caused, by a big crunch. The universe we live in was preceded by another one.

It seems to me that the question whether god exists and whether there is life after death is unanswerable. So far as anybody can tell, there may be something like a god, or there may not. So--yes, it could be a matter of faith. I would prefer to call it a matter of judgement, just as when we are forced to choose between various courses of action with incomplete knowledge. Whichever way you decide, you have to say "probably". This makes religion as we have known it untenable. It also means that we logically *must* respect people with different opinions. (Thank heaven, I'm married to one.) This is not just a matter of good manners but of honesty.

On the other hand, scientific theories current today in physics, astronomy, biology and neuroscience will sooner or later be superceded by others. So our understanding of the kind of universe we are in may change (yet again). Given that we do not know what future discoveries will be made (otherwise they would already have been made), we cannot know what new ideas--if any--about whatever lies beyond the physical cosmos may one day appear reasonable. There have of course been repeated changes in the consensus of theologians, philosophers and the rest of us in the past. Different views have often coexisted. The Romantics rejected the "mechanistic" view of the cosmos derived from Newtonian physics; Newton himself believed in mystery and magic.

What is more, we don't just observe the universe, we feel something about it, there is a sense of something wonderful and supremely beautiful in nature, something beyond our everyday grasp. As a gut reaction, this is a fact of human experience. No matter what our cultural background, we from time to time experience a correspondence between ourselves and the cosmos--perhaps in the stars, or in the hills, or in music: 'there lives the dearest freshness deep down things':[73] an inner rightness in nature and the cosmos. We revere the beauty and vastness of the cosmos. On a clear starry night, we are inspired to invoke an 'I-You' rather than an 'I-It' relationship with the cosmos.[74]

Whether such feelings or intuitions tell us anything about what the world is actually like is another matter. Intense human feelings do not necessarily correspond to the way the world is. Yes--we do have intimations of the divine. But I would suggest that No; we cannot draw conclusions about reality from these.

The Alternatives

So we seem to be faced with the following options. (1) First, the present state of scientific knowledge suggests that we may not have the mental equipment--the language and concepts--to plumb the workings of the material cosmos. This is not only stranger than we imagine but stranger than we can imagine. So we can hardly expect to have the mental equipment to understand things we cannot observe. If we do not have the language and concepts to comprehend the workings of the material universe, can we expect to have the language and concepts to comprehend whatever might or might not lie beyond it? Perhaps, therefore, we should simply admit that there are certain questions we cannot answer--and may never be able to answer; and therefore keep an open mind and relax (agnosticism). Either, we simply don't know at present (mild agnosticism); or, we don't know at present and it is highly unlikely that we will ever be able to know; or, we may be pretty sure that we will never be able to know (strong agnosticism). We shdn't invent answers. Like travellers on a pitch-black night in unknown territory without satnav or a map, we might be best to stick with what we do know, and not make any further assumptions. Our ignorance about the ultimate laws of nature need not have any impact on our lives.

(2) But it might equally well still seem reasonable to some people to make a decision one way or the other about the existence of god and a life after death, based on the evidence we do have. We may be unlikely to get any more convincing evidence one way or the other. After all, we do this in lots of things. If we are lost in a desert or a jungle, we have to make up our minds which way to go. This would be not so much a moral obligation as a matter of common sense. Is "the god question" like that?

(3) Some, however, may think that what we do know about the world we live in from non-religious sources (our life experiences, the natural sciences etc) points, however inconclusively, in one direction or the other.

Thus (3A) some think that what we know signifies that there cannot be a god (atheism).

The trend of scientific discovery in recent times has certainly whittled down (like ice on rock) the scope of what can be believed. Darwinism eliminates intelligent design of life forms; neuroscience explains mental phenomena which previously could have suggested a non-material soul. Time after time, the evidence that appeared to point to the existence of god or life after death has been shown to be explicable in other ways.

That this whole wonderful cosmos, from hydrogen to living cells to human brains, exists on its own without any maker, designer or overseer may seem to many people intuitively unlikely. But we have come across so many counter-intuitive things in modern science that we should not rule it out. It could be one of the most amazing things about the cosmos.

Others (3B) think that on balance what we know indicates that there is some kind of god and perhaps also some kind of life after death. Could one not say that what we do know does not rule out the possibility of something utterly unknown (and unknowable) to us existing quite apart from us, something indescribable. The fundamental components of what we observe may conceivably be beyond the limits of our comprehension horizon. This something could be non-physical. It need not be something that intervenes or has anything to communicate to us.

I don't see why we should just rule this out. What we do know, however, including evolution by natural selection, suggests that, if there is anything apart from this physical world, it is different from anything human beings have thought it was.

Some modern scientific theories, such as relativity and quantum mechanics, are profoundly counter-intuitive. On a very small scale and a very large scale, the physical world is different from what people expected. Does this suggest that we cannot make any reasonable guess about something beyond our field of observation (such as the divine)? Or does it suggest, that the existence of something divine need not be ruled out? Your guess is as good as mine.

Some would say that the divine *can* be inferred from the world as we know it. Some think that the cosmos as we know it by scientific means, and our lives as we experience them, make no sense *without* the divine. Is it not reasonable to infer the existence of something unseen as a means of making sense of, explaining--in the way we explain things in our everyday lives--what we can see?

Does our ignorance justify a leap of faith, then? Since we don't know, aren't we entitled to believe that god does exist and there is an afterlife? If what we know from other sources merely leaves these questions open and unanswered, is it not possible, reasonable, sensible perhaps to make a 'leap of faith'?

Revelation: the Leap of Faith

Most of the religions which people believe in today say their teachings derive from god himself. God has 'revealed' his message about truth and morals to us humans. If this is the case, all we have to do is accept the existence of god, or the possibility of god's existence, and then we can know all other aspects of the truth which religion teaches directly from what he himself has revealed. This is what is involved in 'the leap of faith'.

There are several problems with accepting divine revelation as a guide to the truth. The first is that there are so many alleged revelations saying different things. All religious believers claim that *their* revealed text is the one and only truth. Each revelation is thought by its adherents to be self-evidently true and good (they may also think that those who can't see this are in some way not just mistaken but malicious; or they may not).

But how does one choose between them? The only answer is to invoke something other than revelation, such as common sense or one's own instinct. *Reliance on revelation requires one to step outside the sphere of revelation.*

Some people try to get round this by arguing that the revelations (or most of them) are "really all saying the same thing", for example, that there is one all-powerful, all-knowing, all-loving god and a life after death, and that we should practise justice and generosity. Karen Armstrong has tried to assimilate all the "Abrahamic" faiths (Judaism, Christianity, Islam), on the ground that they all believe in one all-powerful, all-knowing, all-loving god, life after death, and all preach certain similar moral teachings. This is not an altogether new approach. Christians thought their revelation superceded that of the Israelites, but they kept the "Old Testament". Muslims think that Moses and Jesus were bearers of truth, but that their followers had perverted their teachings. This was a topic of lively discussion in medieval Baghdad and renaissance Italy. More recently, theosophy has set out to synthesise the religions of the East and the West. Gandhi was perhaps the most creative example.

On some points, it may be possible to find agreement. Yet Judaism, Christianity and Islam, while they all preach one "god", ascribe fundamentally different kinds of behaviour to him. There are significant differences between the Yahweh of Judaism who gives enormous privileges to a single race, the Christian God who allowed himself to be killed by his opponents, and the Muslim Allah who commands his followers to colonize the earth and to subordinate or kill anyone who thinks differently.

To find agreement between different revelations, one has to use criteria for assessing what is or is not true, what is or is not moral, which come from outside this or that particular revelation. These criteria can only be derived from philosophy and human sensibility.

Revelation requires interpretation. This is as true of statements claiming to come from god as it is about other statements. All believers *do* interpret their sacred texts. They have to, either because the meaning is not clear, or because there are internal contradictions, or because its statements are manifestly false, its commands manifestly absurd or immoral. A sacred text may tell you the earth was created 4,400 years ago, it may tell you never to resist force, or to kill unbelievers. (So it is a good thing believers do give themselves the right of interpretation.)

But if revelation is to provide a way out of our uncertainties, it has to be unconditional, beyond the interference of 'reason'. Once you admit the possibility of error, you are no longer treating it as revelation.

The only way in which anyone can make a reasonable judgement between different claims to be the one and only true revelation is to compare how each measures up to what we know about the world, and ourselves, from other sources. And again, to ask whether they teach what we think of as good conduct. Once one starts judging revelation by criteria outside itself, one is no longer viewing it *as revelation*--that is, as something already given us from outside ourselves, something already out there regardless of what we may think. If we can assess revelation in this way, why do we need it?

The more we learn about nature and the cosmos, the more unlikely it seems that whatever there is out there would make revelations to us. The world as we discover it just does not seem to be like that: it is unbelievably complex and at times incomprehensible--but self-revealing? And it is surely ridiculous, considering everything else we know about nature and the cosmos, the very uncertainty of our knowledge, to imagine that any "supreme being" associated with the cosmos would condemn us to eternal pain for not believing in its existence, or in what it had revealed. Any supreme being which could have been responsible for a cosmos such as ours, would surely require, if anything, intellectual honesty. That certainly is the only way anyone can understand the cosmos and natural world for which such a supreme being would be held to have been responsible.

The alternatives we have looked at are not all mutually exlcusive. The leap of faith may be based on agnosticism but draws a different conclusion. Most believers probably think that there is some evidence for the existence of god and that this is enough to justify faith. But it was much easier to adopt this position up to a couple of hundred years ago than it is now. Yet many would say that it is still possible to do so.

All this helps explain why scientists themselves, immersed in the process of research and discovery, hold different views about religion. Many scientists (Max Planck, for example) have thought that religion and science operate in different spheres and are complementary. In 1927, at a ground-breaking conference on relativity and quantum mechanics, a group of scientists, including Werner Heisenberg, Wolfgang Pauli and Paul Dirac, had an informal chat about religion and science. According to Heisenberg, Max Planck though that "science is, so to speak, the manner in which we confront, in which we argue about, the objective side of reality. Religious faith, on the other hand, is the expression of the subjective decisions that help us choose the standards by which we propose to live and act". Heisenberg later told Niels Bohr about this conversation. Bohr's response was: "I consider those developments in physics during the last decades which have shown how problematic such concepts as 'subjective' and 'objective' are, a great liberation of thought". Heisenberg himself had "the feeling that rationalism is not enough".[75] There are nuances here which are worth bearing in mind.

It has become almost a truism that science and religion are separate and should not be confused. This is not, however, self-evident; in some areas they clearly do conflict, in others they clearly do not. Einstein thought that there was something inexplicable in the mathematical beauty of scientific laws, that "God is somehow involved in the immutable laws of nature".[76]

Are scientists anyway better equipped to answer these questions than the rest of us? Or is "a scientist looking at non-scientific problems just as dumb as the next guy", as Richard Feynman put it?[77] Engagement in any process of research and reflection may, however, give one some feel for the kind of things that can be true in other areas as well. It depends on the individual. Scientists tend to be shy of definitive answers. Darwin was agnostic. The astrophysicist Jonathan Silk suggests that "one may... have to go beyond physics to comprehend the complexities of nature... Humility in the face of the persistent, great unknowns is the true philosophy that modern physics has to offer... Infinity, as revealed by nature, may be beyond the realm of science".[78]

Knowing and Not Knowing

Sometimes you glimpse something out of the corner of your eye and when you look, it's gone. You are left with a feeling of something not quite accounted for. Or, "what you can't talk about you had better keep quiet about", as Ludwig Wittgenstein said.[79] In Christian theology, this is referred to as "the way of negation", that is realising what *cannot* be said about god. Nicholas of Cusa (1401-64), one of the most original and influential theologians of the Middle Ages, spoke of "learned Ignorance":[80] in other words, know what you do not know. What turns out to be the case may come as a surprise. The truth may be banal. (If we want something sexier, try sex or poetry.) If god were a musician, he would be a jazz musician, improvising a lot. "Heaven and earth must pass away. Only musicians are here to stay".[81]

That we don't have ultimate answers is nothing new. "The Way (Dao) that is called the Way is not the Way" (Daodejing 1). Brahman is "beyond what is and beyond what is not" (Bhagavad Gita 13:12); "Zeus, whoever he is, if that is the name he likes to be called by, that is what I will call him" (Aeschylus, Agamemnon, 160-2). "By doubting we come to enquiry; by enquiring we perceive the truth", said Peter Abelard, the founder of medieval Christian theology.

Many mystics and theologians have something in common with agnostics: god is ultimately unknowable and certainly can't be described in human language. Some have spoken of a "cloud of unknowing": we can only know god by not knowing him, by getting rid of all preconceptions about his existence. This is how sufis claim to understand god.[82] At the end of Tolstoy's *War and Peace*, Pierre Bezhukhov is still searching.

We should perhaps remind ourselves that the world is too complicated for any one individual to understand. A huge amount is known but not by any one person, or by any group of persons in communication with one another. There is no superbrain, no possibility of collecting all that is known and pulling it together.

If you are agnostic, you are logically bound to respect the views of others: those who think differently from yourself may in fact be right. The argument between believers and non-believers may be more finely balanced, and more complex, than most on either side are willing to admit. Scientists and philosophers tend not to threaten those who disagree with them. Most religious believers, on the other hand (including Marxists), until recently thought that everyone should think the same as they do, and that if people don't, it's their fault. They are convinced that they and they alone have the correct view of ultimate reality. They have frequently punished non-believers or those who held different beliefs with death or imprisonment.

The Contribution of Religion to our Sense of the World

The World as Poetry

In any case, how does the world revealed by modern science relate to human sensitivity, to our emotions? How does it relate to art and culture? How does it affect our sense of being human? Can we still be lyrical? How can we adjust to our present "known ignorance" (if that is the case) about the nature of the cosmos?

The sense of mystery in nature is common to all humans. The cosmos makes any observer with a brain feel awe. Homer gives us the starlit night as a fact of human observation: "the stars in heaven around the shining moon come clear and bright... the infinite sky is torn apart to its depths" (*Iliad* 8: 555-9). Wordsworth experienced

'a sense sublime

Of something far more deeply interfused,

Whose dwelling is the light of setting suns

And the round ocean and the living air

And in the mind of man'

(*Lines composed above Tintern Abbey*).

The same stars as Homer's shepherd saw made the Catholic Gerard Manley Hopkins think of God.

'I kiss my hand to the stars, lovely asunder

Starlight, wafting Him out of it, and

Glow, glory in thunder...

Since though He is under

The world's splendour and wonder

Yet His mystery must be instressed, stressed,

For I greet Him the days I meet Him and bless when I understand'

(*Wreck of the Deutschland*, verse 5).

One of the greatest physicists declared that the truths shown us by science are "far more marvellous... than any artists of the past imagined! Why do the poets of the present not speak of... the immense spinning sphere of methane and ammonia?"[83]

One ancient Roman poet, Lucretius (c.99-c.55 BCE), did something like that two thousand years ago. Lucretius expounded the atomic theory of the cosmos which had been developed by the Greek scientist Democritus (c.460-380 BCE) and adopted by the Epicurean school. In his poem "On the Nature of Things", he celebrated a purely material universe made up of atoms, in which gods, if they exist at all, couldn't care less about us humans. Streams of atoms pelt through space. "With what speed of movement... the particles that generate matter (genitalia materiai)... (rush)

65

through the vast void" (ii.62-5). This almost conveys an impression of the speed of light, which in fact Lucretius suggested is composed of particles.[84] In "infinite, empty space, innumerable seeds, driven by perpetual motion, fly in all directions throughout the unfathomable universe... The seeds of things, spontaneously clashing together pointlessly and by chance, eventually combine into what, suddenly thrown together, become the beginnings of great things, of earth, sea, sky and living species" (ii. 1053-63).   For Lucretius nature throbs with lyric sensuality. When spring comes, "the soft painted earth pushes up the flowers, the oceans smile, the heavens, grown still, glow with a diffused light" (i:7-9); then young lambs, "their new-born minds drunk on neat milk", frisk voluptuously (*lasciva*) through the grass (i.260-1).

Thus Lucretius shows that a scientific explanation of the cosmos based on particles, waves and bosons, could be material for poetry. His universe is godless yet sensuous. How bald, absurd, unpoetic is the book of *Genesis* by comparison! The author seems insensitive to the thrills of nature. But scientists today don't write poetry, and poets aren't as interested in science as they might be.

For an agnostic, all is not doom and gloom. One can have poetic feelings for nature and the cosmos with or without religious belief. We can have a relationship with being that is at root loving. In our own lives, we experience both science and poetry. Science, poetry and art went hand in hand in classical Greece and ancient China, the Renaissance, the European Romantics,[85] the age of Einstein and Picasso.

Religion as Myth

We may see religions as metaphors, allegories, myths. This is what the Buddha did. He thought his way through and out of religious beliefs. That is how Christians read some of the Hebrew Bible. So let us see Hindu, Judaic, Christian and Muslim scriptures as stories which whisper about our existence. The first time I stepped into a mosque, I had the feeling of the utterly other: god is *not* here. This is a way of sensing that ultimate reality is inconceivable. The idea that god was born into this world as a child of ordinary parents is not meaningless. As someone said 'it's a lovely story but why did she have to be a virgin?'

If you lived in a valley surrounded by mountains, and one day went over those hills, and discovered another country, you would not forget your birthplace. You would not cease to cultivate its slopes and wonder at its beauties. The priest who was most patient with my stupidities, now sits beside me in the Humanist Society. At 88, he still visits the old and the disorientated every week.

Even if one does not believe in reincarnation, one can see something of the relativity of our lives in the Bhagavadita. The death of Jesus shows how humanity can be preserved in the most terrible circumstances. We could strive to live *as if* the Gospels were true.

The clash between religion and science ceases to be a problem if religious beliefs are read as poetry, metaphor.

It is better for our own satisfaction here and now--and for the environment--if we do not to try to have it all now. It is better to see our lives as repeatable experiments because that way we won't be so disappointed. Of course, from the genes' viewpoint, that is what our lives are.

Myths can tell us something about what the cosmos, the human universe and our inner spaces are like. They convey a sense of the vastness of the universe and of time. The religions of India present whole cycles of destruction and rebirth, each lasting millions of years. "I sit once and plumb whole aeons, see through heaven and earth empty", said the Chinese Buddhist poet Li Po (701-62) on visiting a Buddhist master in his mountain retreat.[86] In Norse legend there was a huge rock in the far north, a mile high, a mile long, a mile thick: once every thousand years, a bird flies up and sharpens its beak on it. When the rock has worn away, one evening in eternity has passed. Religious myths indicate as nothing else does the strange unique dimensions of our lives. They point to something bigger than "me" or even "us".

Are god and the afterlife metaphors for something? Is "god" something without which the human universe does not make sense? Sometimes, one may substitute "humanity" for 'god': for example, "Trust in--", "--will not let you down", `'" seek refuge in--". If so, god is not as unimportant as some suggest. In an extraordinary way, religions succeed in constructing a beneficial superstructure on an imaginary base.

The "awakened mind" of the Buddha, the "holy spirit" of New Testament are accessible to us regardless of what we believe or do not believe. The kingdom of heaven is a state of being.

In Grossman's *Life and Fate*, the hero feels 'a sense of lightness and purity. He felt calm and thoughtful. He didn't believe in God, but somehow it was as if God were looking at him... Nothing could take away his sense of rightness now' (p. 697). A Moroccan who was imprisoned for twenty years in total darkness came to feel "God had not abandoned me. Death could come; as for suffering, I tried to consider it as a minor affair, something to be overcome. Powerful, unshakable, such was my faith. It was detached, by which I mean pure".[87]

Is there within humans something which no individual or community could have invented, and which commands absolute allegiance? Something which takes us beyond our selves; a place where we can find rest when everything else looks fragile and hopeless? In other words, is god inside us? Not inside any particular individual but a potential in the human brain; like compassion, which is not so much innate as growing out of what is innate. It produces as it emerges a feeling of happiness and fulfilment. Those who externalise this "something", making it the creator of the cosmos, may be mistaken, but so are those who deny it altogether. It can be "out there" in the sense that it exists in other human minds too. You don't have to bow down, just keep looking.

Would you feel better for some *thing* speaking or listening to your soundings? Why not just listen to the harmony of life, accept the awe of what is? This world of particles and waves is wonder enough. You are not alone; many others have shared your thoughts and feelings. You may find others here and now who feel the same. We are together in these "silent eternities, these infinite spaces". It is something if you can see it and tell it like it is.

All living beings look for things without knowing exactly what they're looking for. The mind, like a primitive life form, is inchoate, wandering, uncertain, feeling its way. But we can only make discoveries if we are prepared to leave unanswered questions which cannot be answered.

It may be difficult, perhaps impossible, to make sense of ourselves without the idea of something bigger (it doesn't have to be a person), parameters unseen and greater than our own, something that we may be barely aware of, certainly unable to capture or pin down, or to define in any way; of some end or purpose which is not just my decaying body.

There is an underlying wonder and we will never know what it is. We are part of something big, but we don't know what it is. Does not the thought that it did not have a creator make it even more wonderful? James Hutton (1726-97), one of the founders of geology, sits--in the portrait in the Scottish National Portrait Gallery--with an expression of affectionate attention and focussed astonishment. The world is not just particles and waves. Is it a poem? We have to access it, hear it.

Looked at in one way, living beings exist because they desire life. Even though we don't live for ever, most of us would not want never to have lived. Nearly being knocked over by a car is a metaphor for our lives. It could so easily have been different, or so easily not have been at all. Conscious beings enjoy being conscious; intelligent beings enjoy being intelligent. So we may thank every thing in the universe that it exists, and does not *not* exist; that we exist--and do not *not* exist. "God" is and is not; is transparent; relates to everything that exists; is a metaphor for the indescribable beauty of being.

Death and Climate Change

Old Age

Old age brings clarity: it is only as you grow old and no longer able to do things, that you realise what it is that you have done with your life, what it is is you have not done, which mountains you have climbed, which you have missed. In our society, old age is often viewed as an opportunity for enjoyment and relaxation, deferred gratification after all those years of hard slog. Retirement replaces paradise. Other societies have seen it as an opportunity for development of the mind and spirit. The mind never stops learning.

Enlightenment in old age is a secular purgatory. Your failures in life become increasingly vivid and the paths not taken increasingly frustrating.

Some old people are more open-minded than some young people. Old people have accumulated a huge amount of experience and if they're any good they can pass this on to others before they die.

Death

Whether you are a millionaire or homeless, young or old, married or single, healthy or disabled, you will die. However ebullient you may be, you are no match for the processes of nature. Death brings the same relief to everyone. We are only on a visit to the cosmos.

There are many different types of death: violent, natural, suicide, euthanasia, painful, easy, lonely, surrounded by family and friends. The differences between these are so obvious that they should perhaps have different names.

It would be nice if we could consent to our death, if one could see it as the expiry of a contract (with nature? with god?). We could perhaps agree that we have taken enough from this poor earh, that we have done what we could, that it is right and reasonable for others to take our place now as mouths, hands, brains upon this planet; if we could agree that we have had our turn and that now it is indeed someone else's. We don't want to clog up the system. We need have no regrets. Remember that nothing immortal has ever been alive.

What happens to us when we die? Who knows? Many say they do know. Some say we live a shadowy existence, as ghostly spirits. Others say we are reborn at another time and place in an endless cycle: who we are depends on who we were in our previous life and how well we behaved. Others say we remain fully ourselves and go to heaven or hell depending on what we have done, or whether we have had the right ideas about god. Heaven is a nice place where all the good people meet up again and endlessly celebrate in the company of god; but Christians think there is no sex in heaven, while Muslims think there is lots of it. Hell is horrible, everyone is wracked by pain throughout their body and by agonising thoughts in their mind. Both heaven and hell go on for ever and ever. Perhaps views of about life after death say more about the living than the dead.

No-one knows they're dead. No living person knows what it is like to die. Perhaps for a split second, death does reveal the shape of things, like someone saying goodbye. The poet John Keats (an atheist), who died at 25 of tuberculosis caught while tending his brother, found death a moment of happiness. So did Gerard Manley Hopkins, a Catholic priest who comforted the destitute during an outbreak of cholera and suffered torments in his mind.

It is more difficult to die than to be born. Pain throws us back on our own devices. When someone dies, 'the universe inside a person has ceased to exist. The stars have disappeared from the night sky'.[88] There is no camaraderie among the dead. Death is an efficient administrator, answers all questions and none. Non-existence is easy. We will experience the twenty-second century just as we experienced the nineteenth. You are in geological time. You return to the vastness of the cosmos, become part of the universal story. The particles of our bodies and minds will still be there, so will children and loved ones, and the cosmos which we loved. So the more we are attached to people and the natural world, the less we need to feel sad about dying, because things so dear to us will still be there.

Mass Murder

We may be prepared to face our own death. But the death of an individual is not the worst thing. Whole families, villages and tribes have been wiped out by disease, a natural catastrophe or other human beings. This has happened time and again throughout history. It is estimated that about 70,000 years ago a natural catastrophe all but wiped out the entire human species; it seems that only a few hundred survived-- just about enough to continue suuccessful breeding. 700 years ago the Black Death wiped out about one third of the population of the Middle East and Europe.

Both instinct and habit have conspired to make humans compete fiercely with those seen as outsiders. Archaeological evidence suggests widespread killing, massacre even, as a regular behaviour pattern amongst early humans, when it came to dealing with those outside one's own circle. Chimpanzees treat rival populations in much the same way.

This dynamic lies behind the history of tribes and states, and international relations today. The instinct of groups to compete with one another is reinforced when the other speaks a different language, looks different or practises a different religion. It is amazing how quickly the competition between 'Communism' and 'the free world' was replaced by that between 'Islam' and 'the West'. A gap was waiting to be filled.

There is a grim rationale to the mass extermination of humans by humans. Early humans were hunter-gatherers living in kinship groups of about 100. When a group grew beyond a certain size, some may have hived off to form another group. This would work so long as there was territory to spare. This was how humans spread across vast areas of the globe, along nutrient-rich coastlines. One route would take them from subtropical Africa across the Red Sea on to India and eventually Australia.

But when the population of a region outstripped the food supply and there was nowhere to migrate to, rival groups had to compete for territory and resources. It was 'natural' for groups based on kinship to get rid of rival groups, if necessary by slaughtering the males, including children, but keeping the females as breeding partners. This 'genosorption', as E.O. Wilson calls it,[89] appears to have happened quite a lot. Homer (writing around 700 BCE about a period some 400 years before that) speaks of it as if it were a common practice.

Mass exterminations on a larger scale took place during the unification of China in the third century BCE, and the Mongol invasions of Eurasia in the thirteenth century CE. These were killings on a scale never seen before, far beyond what was necessary just for survival; motivated perhaps by "reason of state", military strategy, revenge or hatred of people who spoke a different language and worshipped different gods.

Nowadays such behaviour is treated as criminal or insane (Nazism and Communism, for example). Most civilized people nowadays could not conceive themselves capable of such acts. Buddhism condemns the killing of other humans altogether.

Yet in recent times the aborigines of North America and Australia were exterminated as a matter of calculated policy by European immigrants. This was done for territory and resources. If the aboriginal inhabitants were to go on using the land for hunting, for example, the European immigrants would not have been able to develop it for pasture and agriculture. Under Stalin, the government of the Soviet Union regarded the deaths of millions by famine and deportation as an acceptable side-effect of state planning and economic development. The British government did nothing to prevent mass deaths by starvation in Ireland during the 1840s, or again in India as recently as 1942. This was justified on grounds of economic or strategic policy.

Today, the death of millions through starvation, disease and malnutrition could be prevented by people who are themselves living in comparative luxury (and complain about it). Perhaps a billion humans live without clean drinking water or sanitation, worn out by war and disease. Millions are still dying as little babies, unfulfilled, having hardly experienced life at all.

Large-scale exterminations of humans by other humans have been undertaken for the purely human motive of religion or ideology. The most glaring example was the extermination of Jews and others by the National Socialist government of Germany between 1940 and 1945. This was deliberate, systematic and arbitrary killing without precedent in evolution or history. But it is part of human experience.

Today we are faced with the prospect of a mass killing of humans by humans on an even larger scale, and possibly the extinction of the human race, by nuclear or biological weapons. Hundreds of thousands or even millions of people--and, conceivably, the whole human species--could be destroyed at any moment by nuclear or biological warfare. States, such as the one I live in, stockpile such weapons as a safeguard against other states using them against us. For this to be a genuine deterrent, each state has to be prepared, or look as if it is prepared, to use them.

This is different from anything we have been faced with before. The technology now at our disposal means that behaviour patterns related to the way we are, the way we have evolved and learned to live, can have disastrous effects which no-one has calculated or intended. Or at least, not quite.

Nuclear or biological war could be triggered by a desperate or even insane leadership; or by accident. Nuclear or biological weapons could be captured by terrorists, who might bring into their calculations the prospect of getting eternal reward in heaven for themselves and sending their enemies into eternal hell. They might be prepared to use them regardless of the obvious consequences, because they believe it is right, in god's eyes, to pursue their goal despite all else.

Climate Change

Today, we face the prospect of another sort of mass killing, not deliberate but avoidable, through global warming due to the emission of greenhouse gases (GHGs). This could kill millions, perhaps billions, of people, and conceivably exterminate the human species.

Unlike biological or nuclear war, it is not something whigh *might* happen. It is something which is *already happening*, not because humans actually want to kill other humans but as the predictable result of things that we are doing. Not every individual may be aware of this, but they could be and perhaps should be. These deaths will be a result of what humans have already done, are continuing to do as you read this, and show no sign at the present time of stopping doing.

This may turn out to be the finale of humans' relationship with the cosmos. It shows us what it means to be human. The prospect of it ought to inform how we live.

A catastrophic change to the earth's climate through human action is something which no previous generation has had to contemplate. No previous generation has had to face the possibity that the entire human species may be wiped out. People had visions of the end of the world as something that might happen in their lifetime. But this is the first time that there has been hard evidence of the possibility of the extinction of the human species. (Religious beliefs in an end of the world soon to come may have been just as convincing to those who held them as calculations based on scientific evidence are to us. But they held out the prospect of something better to come.)

The effects of global warming, though they are being brought about by what we are doing now, may not be noticeable for some time. Whereas a nuclear or biological disaster could happen suddenly and unpredictably--or not at all--the effects of global warming are gradual. They may not yet be apparent to most people, and by the time they do become sufficiently apparent for people and their governments to be prepared to take serious action, irreversible damage may already have been done. The full effects of what we are doing now may not be felt for a generation or two.

The Facts

The fundamental facts about global warming were established within the scientific community by the late 1970's. "(T)he evidence as it stood in the 1970s was adequate to pronounce a relatively strong conclusion, according to the usual standards of scientific discourse. If the question... were of purely academic interest, it woould have been considered provisionally settled at that time".[90]

The best available accounts of the consensus among scientists from all over the world today on the effects of greenhouse gas emissions are the reports of the International Panel on Climate Change (IPCC), the most recent of which was published in 2013. These reports examined the causes and effects of climate change and suggested the best courses of action to minimise its harmful effects.

Over the last century, the earth has become about 0.8°C warmer. Practically all scientists agree that this is due to an increase in the concentration of greenhouse gases, such as carbon dioxide (CO_2) and methane, in the earth's atmosphere, and that this is caused by human activity. Greenhouse gases prevent the sun's heat escaping back into space (the 'greenhouse effect'). Atmospheric concentrations of CO_2 were c. 280 ppm in 1750, before the industrial revolution; they have recently exceeded 400ppm, and are rising at a rate of about 2ppm per decade. In previous hot epochs, overall warming was 5°C; the present warming could be anything from 2°C to 10°C. But the earlier rates of warming were very, very much slower: 0.000025°C per 100 years during the Cretaceous, 0.025°C around 56 million years ago, compared with 1°C to 4° at present. This made it much easier for species to adapt.[91]

Scientists agree that this increase and the consequent global warming is due to the burning of fossil fuels (coal, oil and gas) by us. All living things on the planet contain carbon compounds which, after they die, are stored up in their corpses on or beneath the ground. Whenever we use fossil fuels, these are released back into the atmosphere. Carbon compounds emitted by decomposed animals and plants, which took hundreds of millions of years to accumulate, are now being released within a few decades.

Estimates for the future depend upon how much greenhouse gas we emit, that is, how much fossil fuel we burn, from now on. This puts the spotlight on the measures we take--or do not take--to burn less.

It is generally thought that, in order to prevent the physical environment of our planet becoming so degraded as to trigger serious economic and social collapse, we have to keep global temperatures at no more than 2.°C above their 1990 level. This probably means that we should keep the amount of CO_2 in the atmosphere at or below 450 ppm. James Hansen, one of the leading authorities on climate change, thinks that a maximum of 350 ppm, giving a rise of just 1oC above the 2000 level, is the only safe bet.[92] We passed this long ago.

It is therefore crucial that emissions peak, and we start *reducing* the amount of greenhouse gases we pump into earth's atmosphere very soon indeed. If this had occurred before 2015 (which is now impossible), we could have contained the rise in global surface temperature within what are widely regarded as safe limits, between 2°C and 2.4°C above 1980-1990 levels. "Global emissions would need to peak between 2000 and 2015" if we are to keep below the +2° and +2.4° limit. According to the IPCC and many other scientific sources, the consequences of this would have been manageable: human life on earth could have continued more or less as it is now, without painful disruptions.

Some scientists have estimated that we can only achieve a limit in the rise of global temperatures to between 2°C and 2.4°C if emissions drop to *between 25% and 40% below 1990 levels by 2020, and by much more after that*. And this is clearly not going to happen. Others take the more pessimistic view that, even if we just stopped *increasing* emissions *today*, it is likely that over the next few decades global temperatures will rise by as much as 2.4°C.[94]

The report of the fourth IPCC (2007) estimated that, if we continue with "business as normal", if action is not taken to reduce carbon emissions, until 2100, the concentration of GHGs in earth's atmosphere will have risen to between 600 and 1550 ppm.[95]

In fact, of course, emissions, far from peaking, in accordance with the IPCC's 'safe' estimate, by 2015 at the latest, are increasing, and at an ever growing rate. They rose by 31% between 1997 and 2008.[96] According to the 2013 IPCC (as reported in *The Economist*) '(b)etween 2000 and 2010, greenhouse gas emissions grew by 2.2°C a year--almost twice as fast as in the previous 30 years'.[97] They are currently 47 billion tonnes a year. The annual emission increase reached a new record level in 2007, and, under business as normal, the 2007 IPCC projected an increase in global greenhouse gas emissions "from 25% to 90% between 2000 and 2030".[98] In fact, as the 2013 IPPC reports, governments are nowhere near achieving their stated goal of keeping global warming below 2°C (above c.1990), and are falling further behind. The 2013 "summary for policymakers (SPM)", even after it had been heavily doctored by politicians, concludes that "the world will pass a 2°C temperature rise by 2030 and the increase will reach 3.7-4.8°C by 2100, a level at which damage, in the form coastal cities, lost species and crop failures, becomes *catastrophic*".[99]

Even after both the effects of carbon emissions on global warming and the consequences of such warming for human and animal life became well known, emissions, far from being reduced or remaining static, rose. Long after the problem became clear we have continued to make disasters more likely to occur.

The inertia of the climate system means that it takes a while for surface air temperatures to respond to increased amounts of greenhouse gases in the earth's atmosphere. And it takes even longer for increases in surface air temperatures to penetrate the ocean depths. Temperatures will continue to rise *even after we have started to reduce our emissions*. This is because "many greenhouse gases remain in the atmosphere for thousands of years".[100] The last time they were at such high levels, it took about 100,000 years for them to dissipate.[101]

The fact that the effects of our actions are so massively delayed obviously reduces the incentive to act now. Such a time lag between emissions and their effects is a major problem in stimulating effective action to deal with global warming. Those living now may not be seriously affected. Our children may well be. The outlook for our grandchildren is certainly bleak.

The effects of greenhouse gas emissions continue long after the emissions themselves have been reduced due to *positive feedbacks*. The amount of global warming to date *has already* given rise to significant feedbacks. These make the process of global warming close to irreversible, at least until the amount of greenhouse gases in earth's atmosphere has decreased significantly. And this, as we have seen, is not going to happen for thousands of years.

In the words of James Hansen, "feedbacks are the guts of the climate problem".[102] For example, ice sheets reflect the sun's heat back into space, thus acting as a buffer against global warming (just as it is better to wear white clothes in a hot climate). But, as ice sheets melt due to the global warming which has already taken place, the increased area of clear water retains more of the sun's heat. Morover, warmer oceans absorb less carbon dioxide. Again, under normal conditions, plants and the soil soak up carbon dioxide; but, when stressed by high temperature and drought (as occurred in Europe during 2003), they *emit* carbon dioxide. During 1998-2002, over a billion tonnes may have escaped into the atmosphere from this source alone.

But perhaps the most dramatic, indeed potentially catastrophic, feedback is the release of the vast amount of methane locked up in the permafrost and on the ocean beds. Methane is a more potent greenhouse gas than carbon dioxide. Now, an estimated 500 billion tonnes of carbon are locked up in methane in the Arctic and Siberian permafrost. "By the end of the 21st century, the area of permafrost near the surface (upper 3.5 metres) is projected to decrease by between 37% (according to one model) and 81% (according to another model)" (2013 IPPC summary for policymakers, p.23). The permafrost has already begun to melt, partly because global warming produces a larger rise in temperatures in higher than in lower latitudes. It has recently been discovered that, between 2002 and 2009, methane emissions from the lakes of Siberia and Alaska increased by 45%. It is predicted that, under business as normal, at least 50 billion tonnes of methane will escape from this source alone in the coming decades.[103]

The last feedback to come into effect, and the most potent, is the hundreds of billions of tonnes of carbon locked up on the seabed in the form of ice crystals containing methane, known as methane hydrates. This is where the largest amount of carbon on earth is stored. A change in temperature or ocean circulation could destabilise these and belch out methane into the atmosphere.[104] It is known from geological data that, when planet temperatures reach a certain level, these methane hydrates are belched out into the atmosphere. This effect (of the global warming which is already taking place) will take even longer to occur, because of the time it takes for higher temperatures to penetrate to the ocean floors.

The melting of methane hydrates is the most likely explanation for the biggest mass extinction on record, the Permian extinction of some 250 million years ago, when 90% of all living species were exterminated.[105] (In this case, global warming was probably caused by a series of massive volcanic eruptions; the chemicals released by these dissipate quicker than CO2.) Such a release now "could destroy terrestrial life almost entirely".[106] Or, as the IPCC puts it, "long term unmitigated climate change will 'likely' exceed the capacity of people and the natural world to adapt".[107]

Some scientists think that these positive feedbacks mean that the trend towards catastrophic global warming is *already irreversible*. Once glaciers and ice sheets have gone, they have gone. Only something like another ice age would bring them back--no sign of that just now. Once methane has been emitted into the atmosphere, it will stay there for thousands of years. The core of the climate problem from our point of view is that, by the time people and governments (assuming these still exist) have tangible evidence (as opposed to scientists' predictions) of the effects of increased greenhouse gas emissions, the damage will already have been done. The feedback mechanisms *will already have been triggered* (by us).

There are signs that global warming is taking effect faster than anticipated. "Changes have occurred either at the upper end of the projections or even above <their> range... The great irony is that climate scientists, if anything, have been too cautious and too conservative."[108] One reason for this is that some of the processes producing positive feedback are occurring faster than expected.

The conclusion from all this is that, if we do not start to reduce emissions *immediately*, the rise in temperature looks set to be significantly greater than the "safe' 2.°-2.4°C. Some research conducted since the IPCC report of 2007 suggests that the situation is even more serious than its authors stated: that, given the amount of greenhouse gases already in earth's atmosphere, and taking into account feedback, it is now improbable that the level can be restricted to 650 ppm, which would cause a rise in temperature of perhaps 4° above the 1990 level. The scientist who reported this finding confessed: "As an academic I wanted to be told that this was a very good piece of work and that the conclusions were sound... But as a human being I desperately wanted someone to point out a mistake and tell me we had got it completely wrong".[109] According to the 2007 IPCC, if emissions do not peak until 2060-2090, a temperature rise of between 4.9° and 6.1° is likely. The consequences of this, while difficult to predict in detail, will almost certainly pose considerable risks for most large animal species and for many if not all humans.

So we are, if not beyond the tipping point, very near it. "If nothing (is) done to slow climate change, it would, in the long term, be likely that natural, managed and even human systems would be unable to adapt and therefore fail to fulfil their purposes"[111]--perhaps a somewhat bland way of talking about mass extinctions. Hansen has put it more forcefully: unless we stop using coal (the biggest source of carbon emisions) *immediately*, "climate disasters will be a dead certainty".[112] Unless we take action immediately, we should not count on the continuation of human life. Certainly, the longer we postpone action, the harder it becomes and the more it will cost. But, since long after the problem became clear, we have not only failed to act, but, by acquiescing in business as normal, made disaster much more likely.

What does it mean for us?

The effects of global warming on climate in specific instances is notoriously difficult to pinpoint. Many people have already died as a result of famines, droughts and floods which were probably partly caused by global warming. Recent events have "revealed higher levels of vulnerability" than were previously expected.[113]

The 2007 IPCC estimated that, by 2020, between 75 and 250 million people will be suffering from water stress (defined as "when a country uses more than 20% of its renewable water supply") caused by climate change.[114] With a rise of just 1oC (that is, in all likelihood within 10 years from now), up to 250 million people in Africa, up to 1.2 billion in Asia and up to 80 million in South America will be experiencing water stress. A rise of 2.0oC would lead to hundreds of millions facing a shortage of water.

This is largely due to melting glaciers. Since 1960, almost a fifth of the Indian Himalayas' ice cover has disappeared ("I have seen glaciers disappear in my own life", said an engineer in Ladakh recently).[115] Under the current rate of warming, the Himalayan glaciers could shrink from their present 500,000 sq kilometres to just 100,000 sq kilometers *as early as the 2030s*. This will leave some two billion people in India, China and Pakistan short of water. If we continue as at present, Hansen thinks that "most of the world's glaciers will be gone within fifty years".[116]

As ice melts at the poles, sea levels rise, making coastal plains and low-lying islands uninhabitable. This has already affected parts of Bangladesh and low-lying Pacific islands. If we exceed +3°C, it is likely that sea levels will rise by several metres, meaning that parts of major cities (Calcutta, Shanghai, New York for example) would have to be evacuated. It would also lead to the loss of agricultural land and the salination of drinking water.

A large proportion of greenhouse gases are absorbed by the oceans leading to increased acidity. This has already increased by more than a quarter since 1750.[117] This destroys invertabrates, by melting their shells for example, and so affects the food chain on which fish stocks rely.

Recent research shows that "sea levels appear to be rising almost twice as rapidly as had been forecast" by the IPCC in 2007.[118] The Arctic Ocean may be completely ice-free in late summer by the 2020s)[119], or (as the much more cautious 2013 *Summary for Policymakers* states) nearly so by 2050 (p. 23). The Greenland icesheet will melt almost completely with warming between 1° and 4°C (SPM p.27), that is, within the range of present likelihood. It is thinning much quicker than previously anticipated. If this melted, it would over the course of some centuries lead to a 7-metre rise in sea levels.

The ice sheets on the edges of Antarctica have also been thinning and breaking up at a faster rate than expected. There are even signs that the central Antarctic ice sheet, which people thought would be protected by the large areas of ice surrounding it, is beginning to show signs of weakening. If Antarctica melted as well, it would, over a considerable period, lead to an overall sea level rise of about 75 metres.[120]

There would probaby be a loss of rainfall in low latitudes, reducing agricultural production by up to 50%. Up to about 3.5°C warming cereal productivity will increase in higher latitudes; higher warming will lead to a decline there too.

Many animal and plant species have already been threatened by global warming. A rise of more than about 2°C would probably lead to extinction of 20-30% of all animal and plant species; over 3.5°C would be a severe threat to 40-70% of species.

Droughts, famines and coastal flooding will lead to mass migrations. "In 2010-11 alone 42 million people in Asia were displaced by "extreme" weather".[121] A great many of these people migrate to cities already threatened by rising sea levels, such as Mumbai, Kolkota, Bangkok, Jakarta.

All of these phenomena (food and water shortages, rising sea levels, mass migration) will of course increase the risk of conflict. There has already been conflict over shrinking pasture and water supplies in parts of Africa, such as Darfur. But no country will be immune from the social effects of climate change. James Lovelock's (2006) picture of a few surviving groups of nomads wandering from one oasis to another in the Arctic[122] may be a trifle romantic.

Global Warming and World History

The causes of global warming lie deep within human nature. It is the unintended result of billions of actions by billions of humans, following instinctive drives. These are increasingly being satisfied by modern technology made available by science. No-one plans global warming or wants it to happen. No-one is deliberately going about making the planet warmer. No, it is the *unintended result* of our actions.

The causes lie in those very abilities which enabled us to survive thousands of years ago: our large, powerful brains. We were able to manipulate our environment for our own needs. We burned down forests to hunt our prey. Sowing crops meant draining marshes and chopping down more forests. The impact of humans on the global climate escalated when we learnt to unlock the energy stored in deposits of fossil matter left behind by thousands upon thousands of generations of dead plants and animals over the last 500 million years. It was the industrial revolution about 250 years ago that kicked off global warming. We have used coal, oil, gas to power manufacture, transport goods and people, for cooking and lighting, to keep homes and workplaces warm in winter and cool in summer, to run computers and talk to each other. We use electricity (most of it produced by coal-, oil- or gas-fired power stations) in almost every activity in modern life, from railways to ovens, from kettles to lawnmowers and TVs. We have come to rely on an ever-increasing range of gadgets, (washing-machines, dishwashers) for the simplest everyday jobs. (This deprives us of physical exercise.)

We rely on fossil fuels for both luxuries and necessities. Our expectations of comfort, convenience and pleasure have escalated. Whatever counts as a luxury, or as something which makes its owner look good, is desired by everybody; people can make a profit selling them. How do you get fridges or TVs, visit friends or even buy food without a car? How can you visit relatives who have emigrated except by plane? "And when they ask you why we died, tell them that our fathers" took cheap flights.[123] The main reason for global warming is that you and I and most people on this planet have become dependent on all these things and use them almost every day.

The line between necessity and luxury is blurred and ever-shifting. Yesterday's luxuries become today's necessities. The industrial revolution generated an undreamt-of increase in personal comfort and luxury. Today, not having one's own car-- or two per family-- can be extremely inconvenient.

Many of our daily necessities (clothes, for example) and a good deal of our food come from far away. We *could* consume more local food, we could even grow our own vegetables, we could produce more goods nearer home. But we are up against the market and the modern economy. It is cheaper to produce clothes in China than in Britain; and there isn't a great deal of British wine. The "law of comparative advantage" encourages each region to produce what it can produce best and most cheaply. The market generates more and more fossil-fuel-consuming activities.

The human appetite for red meat leads to the destruction of forests to make way for grazing land. Increased consumption of meat, especially beef, contributes to global warming. (Methane is also ejected by farting cattle (and humans).)

From childhood, we are invited, through the media and advertising, to play an ever bigger part in the game of consumption. The aims and meaning of life are presented as physical pleasure and comfort. The traditional word for all this is hedonism, and offerings made to it contribute far more to potential human catastrophe than the burnt sacrifices of our ancestors ever did.

The whole modern economy depends on this; the whole modern way of living is structured around it. All of this is now the "way of life" for developed countries. It is modernity. The world economy depends on it. "Growth" means increased use of fossil fuels. During a depression, the environment gets a break. All economic activity, by small and large firms, by corporations and governments, corrupt or lawful, is calculated on this basis.

Fossil fuels play an essential role in travel, bringing up children, managing housseholds, planning cities. The consumption of fossil fuels is embedded in our everyday life-styles and aspirations, in the way we are. The whole world has become a tourist destination. When the ancient Romans had a banquet, they used a vomitorium, a place to sick up, so they could eat more courses. Civilisation is now a global vomitorium.

All this, you may say, applies only to the developed world. But less developed countries can't wait to catch up. The modern Western way of life has become the goal of every society and almost every individual on earth. Few protest. Extreme Islamists have a point, unfortunately the wrong one.

Modern society ("the West") is based on aspirations which are shaped by inbuilt human drives ("human nature"). Human animal appetites, our need for energy, are the basis of 'market forces'; the economy depends upon the physical and psychological character of humans. Human appetites are further stimulated and channelled by our imagination; advertisements reinforce our needs and stimulate our desires. We use our resoning power mainly to satisfy our appetites most efficiently.

The imminent threat of large-scale disaster and possible extinction is thus the result of instinctive human behaviour. Our fundamental drives are in danger of frustrating themselves and even destroying us. The way we are in the world, our biological and psychological selves, have enabled us to survive and reproduce in the face of many threats. Now they are proving fatal. The drive for carbon-hungry goods arises from deep-seated human urges. Our nervous energy translates straight into carbon emissions.

Thus it is our very abilities, our curiosity and problem-solving skills, which have brought us to this tragedy. *Genesis* and *Faust* were right on this.

Our intelligence has enabled us to manipulate the world to produce food and satisfy our cravings for beauty and luxury; to move out of Africa into Asia and Siberia, the Arctic and the tropics. More than any other species, we can control our environment. Intelligence led to modern science and engineering, and hence the ability to derive energy from fossils fuels.

Human appetite, lust, desire generate behaviour which drives global warming. Thanks to modern medicine, our phenomenal capacity for reproducing ourselves poses a further threat to long-term survival. The human population, currently estimated at six billion, may reach nine billion by 2050. This means more and more consumers using fossil fuels.

Humans have a particularly powerful sex drive. In the past, this ensured recovery from epidemics and wars. Conspicuous consumption leads to sexual success. The elite who run societies corner for themselves land and wealth partly to attract the most attractive females. The more wealth, status and power you have, the more attractive you are to the average female. Islam's permission of four wives is realistically open only to the well-to-do. Some of the earliest literature (the Iliad and the Ramayana) is about sex wars.

Procreation, making the most of nature for ourselves and our children, has become part of the problem. Testosterone never learns. Nevertheless, our brains have provided a solution in contraceptives. But several religions forbid their use.

Our reason and imagination developed as means to satisfy our appetites. Now we need to reverse the order: to use our reason, our awareness of our global-historical situation, to redirect and limit our appetites. We should be able to harness our powers of imagination and calculation to correct these trends and so ensure human survival.

Our reasoning powers tend to focus on immediate, local and ascertainable advantages for ourselves and our group. We calculate profit and loss. It will take an enormous, almost supernatural, effort to refocus these powers to ensure the survival of our species. This is what we have to try to do.

What can we do?

How can we reduce carbon emissions? Human survival now depends more than ever before on our willingness and ability to use our brains. We--everyone--need to apply our intelligence in two ways. First, we need to be fully aware of the situation we are in; we have to investigate the effects our actions have on our environment. Secondly, if our children and grandchildren are to survive and have a reasonable life, we need to apply what we know to the way we act.

We have a moral duty to find out the facts about global warming. "The gap between public perception and scientific reality is now enormous".[124] Here we depend upon the scientific community. You don't have to be a metereologist to understand the weather forecast. But everyone needs to understand the kind of certainty science can achieve. I do not understand why, on the issue of climate change, so many are unwilling to accept what the experts know. There is no other field of enquiry in which so many people remain sceptical in the face of overwhelming expert evidence and argument. People seem to be capable of thinking that, because they want the world to be a certain way, that is how it is. There is a tendency to believe what one wants to believe.

There is a clear bias against the notion that global warming is occurring, or, if it is, that this is due to human activity. One finds this time and again when talking to quite intelligent people. This can be for several reasons. Cutting down on the consumption of fossil fuels runs counter to the short-term interests of powerful corporations involved in the extraction and distribution of coal, oil and gas.

Under George W. Bush the US government censored or deliberately misinterpreted scientific data which drew attention to the serious consequences human activity was having on the earth's climate.[125] James Hansen, who since the late 1980's has been trying to present the evidence to US administrations, has remarked on the gulf between scientific method and the method of decision-making by the US government under George W. Bush: when in 2001 a presidential task force heard mention of factors other than carbon dioxide that contributed to global warming, Vice-President Cheney said he would like to hear more about this. "That is pretty much the opposite of the scientific method. In science, you want to examine evidence that seems to disagree with your preliminary interpration".[126]

The media are "free" to say almost whatever they want on this subject. At best, they may put both sides of the case as if these were equally plausible and it were up to the reader or viewer to "make a choice" between the scientific consensus and a few outliers. 64% of people worldwide think global warming is due to human activity, and 61% would approve of action to reduce it, even if this meant harming the economy. But in the US only 45%, and in China only 57% think it is caused by humans.[127] The film *The Day After Tomorrow* and Cormac McCarthy's book and film *The Road* claim to show the after-effects of a cataclysmic disaster, but they avoid any reference to global warming. (They imply instead a deep freeze or a nuclear holocaust, respectively.) Margaret Atwood's *The Flood,* on the other hand, is quite specific about global warming.

Religion, as we have seen, can challenge people to look at things in the round. But it can also direct people's attention to things that don't matter (witness the current obsession with homosexuality in some religious circles); or even make them indulge in petty and pointless wars, which are nevertheless extremely destructive to both human beings and the environment.

While most believers in god no doubt accept the findings of the natural sciences on climate change, a few seem seriously to think that "god" may intervene to prevent any catastrophe that might occur due to our actions.

"God would not allow such a thing to happen". Well, he has in the past. Some think that global warming doesn't matter because such a catastrophe would hasten the fulfilment of god's plan: the destruction of the human species may all be part of god's plan, or the chosen will be snatched up into everlasting bliss. Most people might prefer not to try this on.

But I suspect that the main reason for the bias against accepting that global warming is taking place due to human activity lies in fact that it contradicts our immediate, short-term interests, and that to accept it would imply painful readjustments to the way we live.

Even if the evidence were not as strong as it is, no sensible person would sit back and carry on with business as usual. If we thought that our own house *might* go up in flames unless we took immediate action, even though it was by no means certain, we would take appropriate action here and now and think about it afterwards. If there was just a 1% chance of a gas explosion in your house, you would switch the gas supply off until you had had it checked. You would not leave the gas on just because you wanted to go on cooking and keeping warm. If one were on a plane where most of the instruments were telling the flight crew that something was wrong but some were not, would one be content for the crew to argue among themselves about which set of readings to believe or would one prefer an instant decision to take precautionary measures?

Even for those who do grasp the implications of the scientific data, there can be a gap between what we know and how we behave. This is partly because the consequences of our actions are not yet apparent to our senses, unless we live in places like Bangladesh, the Pacific islands or the Arctic. We are doing harm to others by our actions, but this harm will not become apparent for several years, or even decades. Hence the antennae which might alert our moral faculties--people suffering under our eyes--are not activated.

If our lives or food supplies were being threatened here and now, people would act and expect others to act instantly. Everyone might be prepared to do his or her bit.

Part of the problem about being human today, then, is that we evolved to deal with immediate threats, with things that were going to happen or might happen in at most the next ten years or so. We think that there are more important things for us to do right now: a job, a date. Governments put economic growth before everything else because that's what people want them to do. But in this instance our long-term interests contradict our short-term ones. We know what is going to happen, and we know that we are partly responsible, but this does not affect our consciences as it would if these things were going to happen in the immediate future.

We cannot conceive of a life that we could describe as morally or emotionally good if it was not sustainable; if we could not pass on what we have, the kind of things we enjoy and which make our life meaningful, to the next generation. We would surely consider a life in which we consumed or destroyed things in such a way as to make them unavailable and the planet uninhabitable for future generations, as immoral and unsatisfactory. We could not enjoy such a life in any full sense, knowing that we were irreparably harming others by what we enjoyed.

Life has to be lived in such a way that future generations can continue living on this planet without being too much worse off than we are. This is a moral requirement but it is also a prerequisite of happiness. We cannot enjoy life knowing that our descendants, our children and grandchildren are going to suffer; still less, knowing that vast numbers of people are going to die due to what we in our present generation are doing to this planet. Any "happiness" we had under those circumstances would be hopelessly superficial; it would depend on self-deception, on pretending that what we are doing will not bring suffering to others in the future.

Those who enjoy the "freedoms" of modern market society often look quite miserable. Unhappiness, discontent with oneself, drives people to activities which further pollute our planet. If we are ever to reduce carbon emissions, we are going to have to find other ways of being happy.

But we do not need to harm the planet in order to lead a good and satfisfying life. For family life and friendship, creative work and development of our inner life, we have no need to engage in activities that harm the environment. Everyone can be creative in a way that does not harm the environment. Artists and scientists do not need fancy yachts to make them happy.

Happiness itself reduces our dependence on luxuries that contribute to the destruction of human and animal life. If you're crazy about scientific research, writing poetry or visiting the sick, you don't need so many physical perks to make you happy. You don't need to deforest, deflower the earth.

There is a connection between moral conduct and the Way (Dao). There is a possibility of empathy with what is, with things as they are. Through our mental and emotional processes, we are connected with what is infinite and eternal. Things go better that way, better for ourselves, better for the world around us. We will consider this further in the next chapter.

The commitment to save the world from the worst consequences of climate change, whatever the cost, is the only way we can retain personal integrity, self-respect, a sense of our own worth. It is based on the sense of what it is to be human, of our place as intelligent beings in this amazing cosmos. Even if catastrophic global warming is going to happen regardless of our individual actions, do we want to be a party to this new mass extermination?

If everyone conducted their daily lives in such a way that everyone else could live the same way and life would remain tolerable (possible, indeed) for us all, then the problem could be solved. This would mean taking into account the consequences of our actions for other people on the planet, including future generations. The sad truth of course is that very few are inclined to do any such thing.

Two kinds of action are needed. First, we have to reduce our dependence on fossil fuels for energy. It is possible to produce energy without using fossil fuels by harnessing the renewable powers of nature: wind, wave and water. Fuel can be produced from plants (biomass). But wind is unreliable, and biomass relies on agriculture which is needed for food. The other alternative is nuclear power. This faces problems of cost and safety, including the disposal of nuclear waste. There is a limited amount of uranium in the world; on the other hand the plutonium produced by nuclear fission can be recycled, provided proper precautions are taken.[128] Nuclear fusion would solve all our problems but scientists seem to be nowhere near discovering how to achieve it.

There have been attempts to reduce significantly the amount of carbon emitted by burning coal by means of carbon capture and storage. Again, this is at present beyond our technological capability (or at least doing it cheaply is); it would take years to implement.[129] Hansen, however, holds out the prospect of replacing coal with nuclear power, which he believes is both safe and in plentiful supply.

Tax and subsidies can be used to encourage people to use fuel more economically and efficiently, and to switch where possible to non-carbon sources of energy. This was the strategy of the Kyoto agreement as long ago as 1992 and is part of European Union policy. One can charge people for emitting carbon by building it into the price as an "external" cost (taxing air miles, for example). "It is only through the market that you can get a large enough and rapid enough response."[130] This would involve a considerable change in the way national and global economies are run.[131] Yet "(t)he world could keep carbon concentrations to the requisite level by actions that would reduce annual economic growth by a mere 0.06 percentage points by 2100".[132] All of these policies have to be implemented worldwide if they are to have any chance of success. Otherwise those who implement them will merely be 'subsidising' those who don't.

All these measures are one part of a solution. But we also need to moderate our own use. To develop such technologies on the required scale and to get them implemented worldwide is obviously going to take too long. Meanwhile, not only are more and more people entering the carbon-intensive culture (understandably perhaps) but those already comfortable enough are using more and more.

We can begin with wasteful and unnecessary uses of energy. Strictly speaking, we don't need to use fossil fuels, because time was when we didn't. We used water power for mills, animals for transport, wood for heating; most of the objects fuelled by electricity were simply unavailable. But of course all of this implied massive human labour, some suffering and much less comfort. Nowadays, however, most of us use the energy provided by fossil fuels without a thought for the environmental cost. We need to distinguish between more and less necessary uses of fossil fuels. We need to heat our homes, we have to move about. But we don't need to heat every room to a high temperature, we can travel by bus and train. So much lies in the detail: turning down the heating, switching off the light. We put the heating on instead of a jumper, we travel regularly by air because flights are cheap and convenient. Virtually everyone does it. But we could live without much of it.

We need to limit what is nowadays regarded as normal and legitimate consumption. "Changes in lifestyle and behaviour patterns can contribute widely to climate change mitigation".[133] We have to ask ourselves: if the things that we are doing now are going to make life bad for our children and grandchildren, if our way of life is going to shorten their lives, what does this tell us about how we should be living, about what we should and should not be doing? We have to put the most basic needs of future generations above our own conveniences and luxuries.[134] We need to develop the ability to restrict our consumption *now* in the interests of ourselves, our families, and everyone else's families, *in the future*. This requires long-term rationality, and it is difficult. But how can we dangle our grandchildren on our knees knowing that what we are doing will harm them?

We can only reduce emissions to a sustainable level by making adaptations to the way we live. It seems to be part of the culture today that this is rarely discussed even in otherwise intelligent discussions about global warming. It seems to run counter to the whole tenor of our society and economy.

To be effective, such action to reduce emissions has to combine changes in individual behaviour with changes in public policy. Only individuals can manage the details of their own lives. Every individual, every family, every community, can do their bit here and now, even without any binding national or international agreements. And that would already be setting examples and bringing some influence to bear on public opinion. As individuals, you and I don't need to wait for an international agreement, or for legislation by our own government. We ourselves can choose to eat less beef, insulate our homes, use public transport, avoid unnecessary plane journeys.

We need to moderate our expectations of consumption. More and more people expect to travel abroad by air at least once a year, for sun or snow. Planes put huge quantities of carbon into the upper atmosphere; travelling by plane has been compared to starting a forest fire. It is a luxury we can live without. Nobody needs to travel by air just to have a good time. (If you want to travel by train and boat instead, try www. seat61.com.) The trouble is that a whole industry has grown up around it. Without legislation to restrict it, it is very difficult to deny it to one's family.

Of course action by individuals will not solve the problem on its own. But if it's all we can do at the moment, why not do it?[135] It would maintain our integrity as human beings, and encourage others. Vassily Grossman in his novel *Life and Fate* recounts how a prisoner was forced to help build a gas chamber for the Nazis. He knew that, if he refused, he would be shot, and that the gas chamber would be built anyway. But he refused none the less. Even if the situation was hopeless, we should do whatever we can, however little, to reduce global warming.

But individuals can only do so much on their own; tragedies of the commons hang over us. Most people are unlikely to act unless they know that others are doing so too; otherwise, isolated savings look, and largely are, pointless. We need governments to provide the appropriate infrastructure (for example, reliable public transport). But governments are not going to invest in these areas unless there is strong public demand. Otherwise they will risk unpopularity.

Insulation of homes needs to be done on a scale that will make it relatively cheap. Businesses cannot afford to take measures that will increase their costs unless other businesses do so too. Reduction in the use of private cars requires an improved public transport system.

Human beings have for millenia survived and thrived without modern conveniences and luxuries. Having them is destroying our habitat on the planet. But in present circumstances, people may feel deprived if they don't have them.

We all know the power children's expectations have on those around them. Everyone's lifestyle is hugely modelled on the way they were brought up and what they have been told is important. From earliest childhood we are led to assume that certain things are normal. Peer-group pressure pushes us towards ever more exotic forms of consumption. If only we could forego a few conveniences, a little comfort, so that life for generations to come may be *possible at all*! Is this too much to ask?

It would help if we could find more satisfaction in less exotic things like birdsong, flowers and landscape. If one scanned the brain of someone looking at a flower, I would be surprised if they didn't find as much glow of pleasure as in someone lying on the beach on a tropical island (after the first few minutes).

It would help if we recognised that the kinds of pleasure which dominant forces in society urge upon us (some of which are the prerogative of the super-rich) bring only temporary satisfaction, temporary relief from inner disquiet. To find lasting satisfaction in anything rerquires a certain mental attitude. And if we develop the right attitude, we can find satisfaction in all kinds of places where we did not expect it, without the use of fossil-fuelled energy.

The more we find satisfaction in being creative ourselves, the easier it is for us to live in a way that is environmentally sustainable. Looking at a painting, listening to music, reading a novel can give enormous pleasure, yet they are virtually carbon-free. If we can find fulfilment in friendship and love, we can lead fulfilled and happy lives without taking more than our fair share of the earth's resources. More of this in the next chapter.

We have to manage our sensual, competitive and aggressive drives in new ways. Humans can adapt their behaviour in remarkable ways. We did so long ago when we settled into large heterogeneous societies and stopped killing each other as a way of life.

We are faced with a new kind of moral issue, a whole *new set of moral and behavioural problems* which people have never had to face before. Moralists pay a lot of attention to a just distribution of goods between people living in the present day. But we have to give equal consideration to the rights and needs of those yet to be born. This is long overdue

Global warming has been caused by all humans everywhere. All will suffer because of it. There can only be effective action if people see that everyone else is acting. "What I do won't be any good, unless everybody else does it" (the tragedy of the commons). Otherwise, one is at the mercy of free riders; and our own actions will be largely ineffective anyway. The measures I take will count for little unless you take them as well. Most of us go on merrily burning fossil fuels, knowing perfectly well what damage this causes, partly because they are aware that their action will make little difference so long as everyone else is doing it.

One result of the unique and untested circumstances we find ourselves in, is that we have to learn to co-operate with each other as never before.

We have to undertake global collective action. What we do in our own backyards today affects every human being everywhere tomorrow. The planet will, in the long run, be habitable either for everyone or no-one. To reduce carbon emissions, *all human beings everywhere* have to act. But the prospect of an international agreement to cut emissions looks as remote as it has even been. Those who have contributed to the IPCC reports must be deeply disappointed. Their reports suggest that they expected people, especially those in responsible position, to take on board what they were saying. Some countries, firms and individuals are reducing their emissions. But these are dwarfed by the increase of emissions elsewhere.

Co-operation would of course be much more likely if there were a greater sense of world community. But, despite all we have in common, this seems as remote as ever. The human race taken as a whole seems too remote to most of us, too vast, too amorphous to command allegiance. It is difficult to develop a sense of fellow-citizenship except at the most abstract moral level. We have barely started to learn how to pass from concern for our family or our nation to concern for humanity as a whole.

World-wide human collaboration on matters which affect everyone's daily life requires a massive effort of thought and will, a perception of shared interests, a conviction that, when necessary, all human beings should help one another. The fact is, however, that, however diverse our cultures, we all now share the same basic common interest--survival--in the face of a common threat.

A transformation of outlook on this scale has taken place before, as when we emerged from tribes into states and nations. This involved a transfer of feelings of belonging onto larger groups. It succeeded to a remarkable extent in transferring allegiance and the sense of membership from the small kinship group, in which we evolved, to the nation-state or religious community, for which a sense of identity had to be invented. Although humans evolved to live in small groups, in most parts of the world we have for hundreds of generations operated reasonably successfully in groups of hundreds of thousands, even millions. The new behaviour patterns required for co-operation in these more extensive and anonymous communities were made possible partly by new ideas. Larger social groups were portrayed in sympathetic terms as super-families.

So we have in fact already made the mental adaptation from small groups to large ones, at least to the extent of making common collaborative action possible when necessary. People have developed a sense of community in large groups, ranging from the Islamic *'umma* to the U S A. We have learnt how to co-operate in such groups for the benefit of others regardless of their genetic relationship to ourselves.

Another reason why international negotiations on reducing carbon emissions have so far proved intractable, lies in the very nature of the issue. The changes needed in our ways of living are considerable, and the costs of developing renewable energy enormous. It will take a lot to persuade people to undertake them. This has not yet been done on a national, let alone an international scale. There is a considerable lack of common understanding and shared trust between different sections of the human race. Besides, we cannot see the problem with our own eyes. Only after decades will the effects of present-day carbon emissions become clear. The changes that are needed are so far-reaching that only a crisis will induce people to undertake them. Then it will be too late.

Blessed are the Bacteria

Vast numbers of species have gone extinct in the past. About 250 million years ago, about 90% of all known species vanished. Nature is no kindly matron. Extinctions are integral to evolution. It was partly thanks to the last such mass extinction (about 65 million years ago) that a niche was created for us.

These extinctions were caused by geological activity and meteorites. This will be the first and only time there has been a mass extinction caused by the conscious actions of a species, *knowing precisely what we are doing.*

We are not the first species to make such an impact on the global environment. Bacteria over billions of years created the earth's atmosphere. As they made the planet habitable for complex organisms, so we are fast making it uninhabitable. It seems that only we can have an effect as catastrophic as volcanoes and meteorites.

The prospect of global warming affects the way we think about ourselves, the species *homo sapiens*, what it is to be human. If this is the fate of intelligent life, what does it say about the cosmos? If we go, the universe may have lost its only admirers.

We are dancing on the Titanic. Stefan Zweig described how in 1914 the peoples of central Europe saw life getting better and better; so far as anyone could see, this was going to go on indefinitely. No-one had any idea of the calamities that were about to engulf whole populations. That is how blind we are.[136] Business as normal is like being a good citizen under the Nazis.

If we fail, it will be because we were incapable of controlling our own skills. Our science and technology will have destroyed us.

The worst thing is that there will be no future. No-one will read Homer, the Bible, the Quran, the Mahabharata; no-one will listen to Mozart.

It is possible that bacteria and some insects will survive. Eventually, more complex forms of life might re-emerge, and evolution start all over again. Who knows whether there will be feelings, genius, love, music once more? They might even discover human remains.

How to Live

How, then, can we live? How can we be happy? What moral principles are there for those who do not believe in god or an afterlife? These questions are even more urgent now that we are faced with the potential catastrophe of global warming.

Human Nature

Reciprocity (Give and Take)

Why should we consider the interests of other people? Should we ever put other people before ourselves? We all know that no human being can live in isolation. She or he has to have a family, and depends on other people to provide much of what they need in the way of food, clothing and shelter. You will only obtain these if you provide others with something they need in return. We all have to exert ourselves in order to survive. The kinds of exertions humans go in for presuppose a society in which goods are exchanged.

And you can only live in such a society if people respect each others' persons and possessions. This is both self-interest and justice. And it is a matter of both survival and happiness. In the long run, people will only do something for you if you do something for them. Reciprocity means that we should act towards other people in the same way we would like them to act towards us. We should respect other people's lives, families and possessions because we want them to respect ours. If we don't respect theirs, they will not respect ours.

Respect for other people's lives and property is part of the human condition: rules about this are found in every culture and every civilization. It may be called "natural law", "the social contract" or "human rights". Treating other people as we would like them to treat us makes life better for everybody; it is in the interests of all of us all the time.

Morals are connected with our sense of ourselves, who we are. Reciprocity and compassion are grounded in the existence of other persons and our elementary awareness of those persons.

'I will help you provided you help me" (reciprocal altruism) has evolved among humans and certain other species by natural selection;[137] that is to say, groups which practised it have on the whole done better than those which did not. This is "tit-for-tat": you behave towards others on the assumption that they will reciprocate, but if they do not, you withdraw your goodwill; after that, you do not give them the benefit of the doubt until you have evidence that their behaviour has changed. "Never be the first to defect; retaliate only after the partner has defected; be forgiving after just one act of retaliation"[138]. Games theorists have identified tit-for-tat as the most robust strategy in a variety of situations. Reciprocity evolved among several other species as the most effective means of maximizing benefits for members of a group in which there is continuous interaction.

There may be an immediate exchange of goods here and now: I give you something you need, and in exchange you give me something I need *now*. I give you a pound of jam, you give me two pounds of sugar; I help you over the ditch and then you help me. Alternatively, it can mean that I do something for you today in exchange for something that you will do for me tomorrow; what I do for you will some day be rewarded by something you do for me.

Or again, I may do something for you in the hope that *someone else in the same group* will do something for me, and that you will do something for someone else in the group (*generalized reciprocity*). Social evolution has enabled members of small groups to behave altruistically towards others without expecting a return from that same individual.[139] We know, for example, that, if a group of friends are out on the hills and someone runs out of water, someone else will give them some of theirs, even though they know that person can't give them any. This is because they know that, if they run out, someone else in the group will help them out.

Reciprocity is usually practised among people who are related to each other (kinship groups). We all live in groups. Certain types of group mean a very great deal to those who belong to them. The first and most obvious is the kin group. All humans belong to a nuclear family (parents, children) and an extended family (grandparents, grandchildren, uncles, aunts, neices, nephews, cousins and so on).

It has been demonstrated that in many species, including humans, individuals are not only dedicated to their own survival and reproduction as individuals, but also to the survival and reproductive success of close relatives. This is a development of the theory of "the selfish gene". Individuals are willing to sacrifice themselves for those who share a lot of their genes.[140] This is because by so doing they also ensure that a good proportion of their own genes will survive. It is thus not unusual for people to be willing to risk their own individual survival to save the life of a close relative. This behaviour evolved because children, parents, brothers and sisters share a lot of the same genes, so that "part of them" will survive even if they don't. This thrust is strongest between parents and offspring, and among siblings, where half the genes are shared. Kin-based altruism extends in an increasingly diluted form to grandparents and grandchildren, uncles and nieces, cousins, and so on.

John Keats was walking in the Scottish Highlands when he heard that his younger brother's tuberculosis had suddenly got much worse.

He immediately rushed back to London; and, despite having a severe cold which (as he well knew) made him liable to infection, looked after his brother day and night. He himself contracted tuberculosis and died aged 25. This act of kindness contributed to the early death of one of the greatest poets.

Many societies emphasise the reciprocal debt of children to parents in their old age. But parenting may be better viewed as a gift with no strings attached. Parents are obliged, by instinct and custom, to do everything they can for their children. Parents owe everything to their children, at the very least because the future of their own genes depends entirely on them (which is why they brought them into existence in the first place). So children can best repay their parents by having children in *their* turn. Having children is like writing a book, having grandchildren like getting it published. Reciprocity is also practised among friends who know and respect each other.

In evolution--and in most people's experience--reciprocity and compassion start in the family group and among friends. Early humans, like many animals (including our closest relatives, the chimps) lived and hunted in small groups, many of whom were bound together by a high proportion of shared genes. Human groups had to be of a certain minimum size (perhaps 100 with 20 fully active males) in order to hunt prey and protect women and children against marauders. Hence we evolved instinctive ways of co-operating in small groups.[141]

Humans developed a liking for small groups and a special facility for working within them. Why does a football team have eleven members? It's to do with rapid communication, instinctive collaboration and mutual trust; the same goes for executive committees, cabinets, military and terrorist units.[142]

Hence comradeship among warriors. The willingness of fighters to sacrifice their own life for the sake of the rest of their group enhanced the survival prospects of the group as a whole in conflicts with other groups in which people were not prepared to stick together. Small groups, such as work teams and many early limited companies, can also be a factor in economic growth.[143] There may of course be intense competition between members of such a group but they tend to close ranks against outsiders.

The problem is that in its instinctive and evolved form, reciprocal altruism only functions in small, stable groups, whose members all know each other, are in constant contact and depend upon each other. Whereas other species have continued to live in communities of the same size and type as those within which their social instincts evolved, humans have gone on to develop much larger communities. It is less easy to apply reciprocity when it comes to conduct towards *outsiders*: to relationships *between* families and *between* small groups.

Empathy

Because we are human, we have the peculiar quality of being able to understand what others of our species think and feel: *empathy*. This makes it possible for us to wish for others what we wish for ourselves, to desire the well-being of others. This was the idea of Confucius, the world's first great moral thinker; it is empathy (*shu*) which gives rise to humaneness ('benevolence': *ren*): 'If I do not wish others to do something to me, I wish not to do it to them' (Analects 4:15 and 12:22). This was what was taught by Jesus of Nazareth (*Matth.* 22:39). Empathy is a development of the heightened social skills which are innate in the social brain of humans.[144]

The ability to sympathize with another person's situation and with their suffering, is the *emotional* basis of reciprocity. As David Hume put it, "All virtues which have a tendency to the public good... must derive all their merit from our sympathy with those who reap any advantage from them".[145] Such compassion motivates one to act so as to reduce the amount of suffering in the world. Like reciprocity, it too is based on identifying oneself with other people, and one's interests with those of others; only in this case, by feeling rather than calculating. Compassion or empathy is an exercise of sympathetic intelligence, an ability to see the world through other people's eyes.

There may even be a connection between compassion and eros. Both are about the willingness and ability to understand the inner world of another, to take account of and anticipate their desires. There is no contradiction between lust for another's body and the desire to promote their well-being; there can be a continuum between passion and benevolence. (Jesus didn't get this.) The loved one was a stranger once.

Selfishness and Aggression

This may all sound very nice, but the problem is that, as we all know, some people won't reciprocate. Even people within small groups, or families, do not necessarily reciprocate. They take something but give nothing in return; they may take more than their share. Such free-riders "take advantage of others", they "behave selfishly"; they defect from the social contract.

Competition is found in almost all human relationships and social situations. It becomes especially serious when different groups (tribes, for example) are competing for scarce resources. Nowadays it is widely thought to be one of, or perhaps the, driving factor in the global economy. It too is related to a form of rationality. "Economic rationality" means maximising gains and minimising losses, buying cheap and selling dear.

Greed, lust and hate, leading to sexual exploitation and aggressive violence are no less part of our instinctive behaviour than reciprocity and compassion. They have served to improve our prospects by making us corner scarce resources, get access to as many reproductive partners as possible, and fight vigorously against anyone that opposes us. Some humans, acting on "gut instinct", rob, rape or kill others, randomly or systematically.

Selfishness, greed, deceit and violence are no less ingrained in our species through evolution by natural selection. There can be antagonisms even within families and small groups. Archaeological evidence suggests that widespread killing, massacres even, took place among early humans. The historical record suggests that rivalry and fighting are as much in line with anything we can call an observable norm of human behaviour as reciprocity and morality. Therefore, the principle of reciprocity has to be taken a great deal further than an evolved instinct to be effective in a large group, let alone among humans in general.

Let us return to empathy: a clear understanding of other minds, based on accurate observations and true deductions, is a great advantage when competing or fighting against others. Here success depends on knowing what is going on in other peoples' minds, on an ability to see the world from their point of view. Deception is a factor in human (and non-human) conflicts. Humans have an especially highly developed ability to mind-read, manipulate and deceive.[146] This too relates to our capacity for rational understanding. But rational understanding per se does not lead to moral behaviour.

The corollary of the in-group is the out-group; the corollary of friends is enemies. In common with all social species, we tend to view those who do not belong to our group as potential competitors. The small groups of early human history were the units of survival; they were the essential means by which people coould protect their families and control enough territory to feed themselves. Scarce resources meant that one had to maximise the resources of one's own group at the expense of others. One needed to wrest control of adequate territory for hunting and gathering. Since humans could calculate what they would need for many years to come, and since they were competing with other groups playing the same game, they might even look to acquire more than was required for their immediate needs. This 'territorial imperative' was intensified by agriculture. Now people were investing even more in particular places.

We may see here a clash of rationalities: the competitive and the reciprocal, economic rationality involving competition in a market, and the moral rationality of compassion and co-operation. These are supported, respectively, by the contrasting instincts of aggressive competition for scarce resources in the interests of survival and reproduction, and empathy or fellow-feeling. We all experience this contradiction throughout our lives. The clash between the impulse to co-operate and the impulse to compete, between the approach we tend to adopt towards members of our own group and how we feel about outsiders, is the circle we have to square.

There is a mitigating factor. Alone among all animal species, humans developed the ability to exchange good across group boundaries. This goes back to prehistory. And commerce depends upon peace. The profit motive-- to maximise gains and minimise losses (economic rationality)-- is found in virtually all human societies. This has given humans a motive for replacing territorial conflict with peaceful competition.

There are three ways in which we can square the circle: (1) law and the state, (2) religion, (3) virtue and the good life. These are not mutually exclusive. They may be combined and, even if they are not all combined, (2) and (3) require assistance from (1); while (1) can never function without a measure of either (2), or (3), or both.

Law and The State

(1) The goals of both kinds of rationality-- economic and moral-- can only be achieved if there are rules backed up by coercive sanctions to ensure that people keep their promises, respect one another's property, and refrain from aggressive violence and sexual exploitation. The state enforces agreements by means of laws: rules which are known to everybody and apply to everybody.

Throughout most of human history people have lived without states, in clans and tribes. These had their own ways of enforcing moral behaviour, which worked so long as the community was small and homogeneous. But, once societies became larger and once clans and tribes were intermingled, the experience of both prehistorical and historical times shows quite clearly that informal sanctions are not enough.

In all early human societies, keeping agreements was regarded as the most solemn obligation; breach of contract has been called "the only act that is always and everywhere held to be immoral", perhaps the *only* universal moral principle.[147] Humans seem to have evolved a particular sensitivity to "violations of conditional rules that express social contracts".[148] It is fundamental to legal and ethical systems the world over. Here writing too helped solve humans' moral conundrum.

Contracts presuppose both foresight and reciprocity: to undertake a contract, one has to be able to look into the future and envisage a range of possible situations and their outcomes. One has to understand and acknowledge that others have the same right as oneself to expect that *both* parties will keep the agreement. One has of course to accept the obligation to adhere to what was agreed even when it is to one's own disadvantage.

One purpose of the state is to enforce agreements, and to ensure that those who do not act reciprocally and respect the rights of others, are found out and punished. One needs clear rules, impartial judges, effective punishment: in other words a legislator, a judiciary and a police force.

Laws have been a part of every human society larger than a tribe. Only with a basis of social and economic stability can people achieve what most (all?) regard as happiness. People are generally even willing to accept a certain amount of injustice (in, for example, the distribution of property) in order to gain security for what they do have. "Better a hundred years of injustice than one day of anarchy", says an Arab proverb.

Despite our best efforts to instil reciprocity and compassion by argument, education and religious teaching, both history and present-day experience strongly suggest that human societies would not be tolerable, or perhaps even possible, unless moral behaviour were backed up at some point by coercion.

This was, at the same time, a way of solving the problem of extending reciprocity to large groups by setting up, over long periods of time and with much bitter fighting, what we now call the state. This is what we-- or our ancestors-- have done. The state is based upon an implicit social contract: that is, an agreement among members, for the most part unconscious, to enforce general reciprocity. Through its legal system, police force and judiciary, the state punishes flagrant breaches of moral conduct. This not only punishes the criminal but induces everyone, in those situations in which even the "best-behaved" people may be inclined to lapse (speeding, for example), to maintain ethical standards.

The vast majority of us will only behave well if the incentives to do so are backed up at some point by the sanctions of law and punishment. There have to be reliable means of settling disputes and punishing crimes. Otherwise, there will be vendettas; these may lead to gang wars, and these may escalate into civil war. Such is the experience of some failed states today. However much individuals might want to behave generously, good behaviour will not work-- that is, those who insist on behaving decently will pay a heavy price-- unless at some point defaulters are punished by law (preferably, quite severely). The larger the community, the more difficult it is to spot the cheat, and the easier it is for defectors to avoid punishment. The state is not an optional extra, but absolutely necessary if people are to have any chance of living together, indeed of surviving at all.

Yet states, with their laws and police forces, work only so long as most of the people most of the time keep most of the rules of their own free will. And they only work so long as the vast majority accept the *right* of the government, judiciary and police to enforce rules. In other words, the moral norms of society have to be broadly agreed, however implicitly, and the state's coercive power has to be regarded as fulfilling a reasonable purpose. In other words, the state has to be legitimate.

These legal and political methods of enforcing reciprocity and justice, need to be supplemented with incentives within the minds of individuals, that is by general standards of common decency, or conscience. The two approaches have to go together. You cannot rely on people's goodwill, however much you may instil morality into them, unless their co-operation is backed up in the last resort by physical sanctions. (This was Hobbes' point.) On the other hand, experience has shown time and again that legal coercion cannot function effectively without moral assent and co-operation among the majority of the population. The drug trade is an ever-present reminder of this throughout the West. The alternatives are dictatorship, social totalitarianism, or anarchy policed by gangs and clans (see Somalia). Experience has persuaded most people that a legitimate state is preferable.

This route out of the human moral conundrum via legal and political institutions has worked for many people, but only up to a point. It has not worked all the time, and for some it has hardly worked at all. It has depended upon great resources of ingenuity, trust, patience, good sense and good fortune. This is demonstrated by the history of every civilised community. Compare, for example, the constitutional histories of Britain and Russia.

One irony is that many (perhaps all) states have been established by successful warlords trying to corner property (land), or to make a name for themselves by establishing firm control over a vast population. (William the Conqueror is a case in point.) They are frequently controlled by a few people who use state institutions to dominate and exploit everyone else. The most successful states, those of China and then of Europe, were fortunate in being founded by rapacious warlords but then civilised by intelligent men (followers of Confucius and Jesus for the most part). Some people never get a state at all. If they remain in relatively small tribal groups, they may not need one.

States sometimes collapse. Once significant numbers of people find they can get away with ignoring the state's authority, everything changes (as Thomas Hobbes predicted it would). In the last hundred years or so, there have been improvements in the rule of law and democracy in some places. On the other hand, many human societies have become less law-abiding and more dangerous to live in. In the human population as a whole, people are probably about as likely to get killed, raped, maimed or robbed today as they ever were.

Once human beings live in larger, multi-tribal or post-tribal communities, the alternative to the state is anarchy of the most vicious kind: a condition of insecurity, in which thugs, gangs and the mafia rule. It is impossible to revert to a peaceful stateless society. Once traditional societies have been absorbed into states, they lose the credibility and the skill to manage themselves.

Recent history, in Somalia, the Congo, Afghanistan and elsewhere, has demonstrated yet again--since we tend to forget lessons learned by those who lived before us--that there can be no return to tribal order. As I write, more and more societies are going into moral and social decline: Afghanistan, Somalia, much of sub-Saharan Africa, perhaps Pakistan. Elsewhere, the danger comes increasingly from criminal gangs and dictators, in various combinations, from Mexico to Uzbekistan.[149] When such challenges succeed, inter-tribal, inter-ethnic and sectarian conflicts ensure that there is no security of property, sexuality or life. There can be no culture. Women and children suffer the worst. And such collapses of political order are among the first things to be feared when climate change takes effect.

Hence, nowadays, living without a state is extremely dangerous. One of the least comforting things about the world we live in is that "failed states" are on the increase. States fail for a variety of reasons, some relatively unobtrusive. Mafia-like groups may infiltrate the legal system and corrupt the political process (as today in Russia and parts of Italy and Mexico). Ethnic or religious groups may defy state authority, in the name of some alternative, "higher" allegiance to nation or "god". An example of the former was the Balkans; the latter is even now being invoked, in situations of extreme complexity, in Afghanistan, Iraq, Syria and possibly Egypt. Or the state may simply wither away as armed groups take control of bits of it, as has happened in The Congo.

As we have seen, we all depend for our security on being members of a state. We also, therefore, have specific responsibilities towards our state (like paying taxes), and towards our fellow-citizens on whose general goodwill we rely to keep that state afloat. This usually involves trying to influence public policy, on which so much depends; in other words, "getting involved in politics". "Civic virtue' has been rightly emphasised but alas less and less practised in recent times. In classical Eastern and Western thought, the virtuous person is someone who undertakes public service.

Anyway, the main point is that humans have often succeeded in extending the instinct of mutual support from the clan to the nation-state. They have succeeded in applying the feeling for reciprocal altruism, evolved in clan groups, to the much larger state. There is clear evidence that it is possible for people to develop the sense of a common good-- citizenship-- in communities of many millions. This extension of our natural feelings needs moral and intellectual effort but it can be achieved.

A World State?

But the most serious problem remains that states have always functioned only in a specific area and so have always been subject to attack from outside, and have themselves attacked outtsiders. In short, there have always been wars and civil wars, and so far as anyone can see there will continue to be wars and civil wars. That is not to say that having an imperfect law-enforcing state is not far better than not having one at all.

It is obvious that human beings need a world state just as much as we need local states, and for exactly the same reasons. States are no more likely to be able to resolve their differences peaceably than are individuals. Physical conflict between states, though it can be avoided for quite long periods, is more catastrophic when it does occur than conflict between tribes or individuals. Experience during the twentieth and twenty-first centuries confirms these elementary facts of human existence. Today, such conflict could result in global catastrophe if chemical, biological or nuclear weapons were used.

To resolve disputes peacefully requires an institution with at least some of the characteristics of a state: the ability to make laws and enforce them, to coerce the criminally-inclined, and to enforce agreements. Today, we need world-wide co-operation between the states that exist in order to combat disease, starvation and climate change. Effective measures to reduce carbon emissions (see above) require co-operation from peoples and states all over the world. For this we need some kind of organised international political community.

But at present, given the diversity of peoples and the sheer size of the human race, it is difficult if not impossible to conceive of anything that one could call a world state. If it is to be achieved, people in all countries have to be persuaded of the urgent need for it.

Morality

Morality and Religion

Religions solve the problem of reconciling altruism with self-interest (that is, moral with economic rationality) by reshaping reality in such a way as to make moral conduct rational even in terms of individual self-interest (as discussed in chapter IIIA). They do this by unveiling a dimension of being in which resources for which humans compete (such as property and sex) appear to be far outweighed by resources that are freely available to everyone, provided only that they behave justly regardless of the consequences to themselves here and now: namely, paradise.

Even so, historical and present-day experience suggest that religious teachings and sanctions such as hell, while they may underwrite moral behaviour and so reduce people's reliance on force, are no substitute for the ultimate sanction of physical coercion, reliably delivered by the state. Throughout recorded history, religious belief *alone* has never achieved an orderly society. It certainly does not do so today. The inhabitants of the Middle East are today re-learning that agonising lesson.

Worse still (as we have seen), religions are socially divisive: they tend to discriminate between believers and non-believers, and between believers of different stripes. And remember that, even if there were a society in which a single religion provided a satisfactory basis for social discipline, it would have to interact with other societies in which there were different religions.

Ever since the seventeenth century, Europe--or some individuals and some regimes in some parts of Europe--embarked on a new venture in the intellectual and organisational story of humanity. This was to replace a single belief system with liberty of conscience and toleration of different beliefs. This subverted the holistic or totalitarian type of culture with something radically different. Apart from its merits as a philosophy--recognising our general uncertainties about the nature of things--this system made it possible for more and more people to coexist within the same social and political space, and eventually within the same international community. We call this 'civil society'. Because people who thought differently were now rubbing shoulders, this enabled them to have deeper conversations--and incidentally to do business with one another. In other words, liberalism was the winner in cultural evolution.

Today it looks as if many different cultures are feeding into a new globalised culture. Greece, Islam and Europe developed what have become the universally accepted way of doing science, mathematics, logic and--with numerous variations-- philosophy. The inspiration behind modern music and dance is to a large extent African. China and India developed techniques for enhancing physical and mental well-being. Westerners tend not to know how to stop thinking, which contributes to mental problems. (This may be connected with Socrates' inner voice which told him never to stop questioning.) China and India knew more about how to become, or remain, happy.

Which is more important? Where knowledge of our own minds and feelings is concerned, China, India and Europe have different but not contradictory things to say. They can perhaps teach one another.

Both national and religious affiliations appeal to sentiments that were already familiar: nations claimed a common ancestry, their leaders were father-figures; co-religionists see themselves as brothers and sisters. The problem is that both nations and religions tend to ground their cohesion upon perception of a common enemy. Let us just hope that the absence of a common enemy does not mean that a community of humankind is impossible. We are after all threatened by a common enemy (an impersonal one): climate change. When the species itself is under threat, it would be useful if we had within us some mental and moral stimulus driving us into wider sympathies for the whole species.

Eastern and Western Views

The third way of dealing with the clash between moral and economic rationality, the instincts of love and of hate, is to extend reciprocity and empathy to others who are neither our kin nor our companions; in other words, to develop the moral sense. This involves both reasoning and feeling.

We have seen how we share with all our fellow-human beings the fundamental quality of having a mind. People from all parts of the globe, and from many different cultures, contribute to our understanding of what it is to be human. Today the scientific community is self-evidently global. We may develop friendship with anyone from any part of the globe. At root, we have or can have as much in common with people remote from us in birth and culture as we can with our own kith and kin.

We saw that, under certain circumstances, it is in our own interest to reciprocate; that is to say, moral and economic rationality coincide naturally or spontaneously up to a point. The emotional basis of reciprocity is empathy: the ability to see and know what another person is thinking, and to sympathise with their situation. Confucius and Jesus equated morality with reciprocity and based it on empathy, the ability to see another's point of view. These have been evolved as part of human behaviour and have been in operation throughout our history, though only within certain limited contexts. But Confucius and Jesus went further: they universalised reciprocity and empathy to apply to our relations with *all* other human beings. Humane behaviour is based on the perception that another person has a point of view as well, and that the world may be viewed from that other person's point of view. We may call this sympathetic reciprocity. Morality develops this empathy and extends it to our relationships with all human beings everywhere.

The idea that moral obligations apply in our relationships with all human beings, not only with our kin or our fellow-countrmen, was suggested in ancient Greece and China about two and a half thousand years ago. It emerged out of the first systematic enquiries about right and wrong. Here we have one case of a complete agreement betw 'eastern' and 'western' thinking. But how can we justify this?

Mozi, writing in China some two and a half thousand years ago, argued that it accords with our human nature as we observe it, and also with enlightened self-interest. He argued roughly as follows: "One who loves will be loved by others, one who hates will be hated by others". Again, you can only persuade other people to treat *your* parents well if you treat *their* parents in the same way as you treat your own. You can only make outsiders treat *your* village well, if you treat other villages well. And you can only expect other regions and states to treat yours well if you treat them well. In other words, we should respect other people's lives, families and possessions because if we don't, they won't respect ours. Thus it is possible to extend universal love ("impartial caring", he called it) to everyone. So one should value *all* other persons, regardless of kinship or status, just as one values oneself.[150]

So Mozi argued that a*ll* human relationships between *all* human beings throughout the world should be based upon reciprocity; and this is possible because reciprocity is a general trait of human behaviour. It is both in our interests and in accordance with our nature. "When there is rightdoing in the world, we live, without it we die; with it, we are rich, without it poor".[151] This is the only way to secure peace. Besides, this is the way Heaven behaves, and that should be our model.

Cicero, writing at Rome in the century before Christ, reached exactly the same conclusion as Mozi, and he too argued from the perceived pattern of human sentiments. Love, he said, "gradually seeps outwards, first to blood-relations and in-laws, then to friends [and] neighbours, then to fellow-citizens... and finally it embraces the whole human race". Such human "affection and association" provides the emotional incentive for moral action. Like Mozi, he argued that friends, family, citizens "and finally everyone (since we want to be one human community) is to be considered for their own sake" (*Laws* I.27-31). As Marcus Aurelius (died 180 CE) put it, the basic character of humans is to "show goodwill to his own kind": "Men are born for of each other".[152] Once again, there is agreement in principle between thinkers of East and West.

These ideas were developed in the modern West by Jean-Jacques Rousseau (1712-78) and Immanuel Kant (1724-1804). Rousseau based the idea that you should behave towards others as you would wish them to behave towards you (general reciprocity) as "a pure act of understanding in each individual, in the silence of the passions, concerning what a man can demand of his fellow and what his fellow can demand of him".[153] Kant explained this act of understanding as the 'categorical imperative':

we cannot understand, make sense of or function in the world without it. It is a necessary part of human consciousness, like space or time. Such categories enable us to make sense of ourselves and the world around us. He expressed the idea of reciprocity by saying that one should always act according to principles which you would be willing for everyone else to act on. We should keep our promises and pay our debts because, if everyone started breaking promises and refusing to pay debts, no-one could believe anybody else, there would be no such thing as a promise. This would make life in society, that is to say human life, impossible. In other words, certain moral principles are inherent in the condition of being human. This was perhaps the ultimate defence of moral rationality, and the ultimate argument for overriding economic rationality whenever it goes against a moral principle.

And indeed we do find that we can have reciprocal dealings with a complete stranger, and that these can generate the same warmth that we feel within the family or amongst friends. This was made graphically clear in Jesus' story of the "Good Samaritan" (ie the good stranger), who helped a badly wounded man after those who were supposed to be close to him had "walked by on the other side".

David Hume placed special value on the sentiment of benevolence because of "its tendency to promote the interests of *our species*, and bestow happiness on human society".[154] The author of the theory of evolution by natural selection held exactly the same view: "As man advances in civilization, and small tribes are united into larger communities, the simplest reason would tell each individual that he ought to extend his social instincts and sympathies to all members of the same nation, though personally unknown to him. This point being once reached, there is only an artificial barrier to prevent his sympathies extending to men of all nations and races." (Darwin, c 1882)

So far, we have been deriving the argument for morality, for a certain set of moral values, partly from the way human society and human social conduct has evolved. The practice of reciprocity and the feeling of empathy, though evolved for small groups, can be extended to large groups and humans in general without violating or asking the impossible of human nature. But this does not mean that moral values bear any relation to the way nature as a whole--the cosmos--is. Morality is based upon elements of our human nature, but it can function independently of any scientific laws or cosmology. There may be no connection between the way the cosmos works and the way we behave; we don't need one. Morality, we have argued, in no way depends upon a beneficent deity. (Naturally, it might be nice if there was some connection.)

This point was put concisely and elegantly by the philosopher-emperor Marcus Aurelius. In his day there were rival views about both the nature of the universe and how we should behave. Stoics believed the universe was ruled by a providence for a purpose, guided by a beneficent deity, and that moral principles are embedded in the structure of nature, humans included. Epicureans, on the other hand, held that the cosmos was a random collection of atoms, which happened to have come together in a certain way by chance, and that the gods couldn't care less. So when we die, we may either be re-absorbed into the Whole (the Stoic view), or scattered as atoms once more (the Epicurean view). Nevertheless Marcus insisted that this should not affect the way we behave. 'As to the Whole, if god-- all is well; if haphazard-- don't you be haphazard too'.[155] The world of nature may be arbitrary and cruel, but this does not mean we have to be so. Where philosophy ends, choice begins.

As individuals, we all die. But we desperately want to connect with, have a relationship with, something which will last when we are gone, something outside ourselves. The most obvious way to achieve this is biological reproduction. But *any* other human being may outlast us. Therefore, insofar as we are connected with others through compassion, they will carry something of us with them into the future. Something of ourselves, or connected to us, will last even longer if we develop a compassionate relationship with other species.

Compassion brings peace, both between people, and within ourselves. The more we really care about the well-being of others, the less we are subject to the kind of anxiety which comes from caring too much about ourselves, from over-calculating our own interests

and I pray that I may forget

These things that with myself I too much discuss

Too much explain (T. S. Eliot, Ash Wednesday I).

We will care a bit less about whether we have paid a bill or how our investments are doing, or even (perhaps) whether X loves us. Compassion is de-centering. It takes the focus away from myself onto what is outside myself, and it does so by way of human *feeling*.

The sense that some ways of acting are right, others wrong, appears to be something which all humans have in common (even though, as we shall see, our understandings of right and wrong, and the ways we apply them, differ). The ancient Greeks, who travelled widely and were more curious about other people, and perhaps more respectful, than (say) the Hebrews or the Chinese, noted that all races had rules about murder, theft and so on, however much they might differ in detail about how these should be applied. Morality constitutes, as it were, the grammar of behaviour for speaking intelligent beings.[156] This point was powerfully made by Mengzi, a Chinese philosopher of the 4th century BCE: "every man possesses the mind of pity... every man possesses the mind that distinguishes right from wrong... Benevolence, propriety... are not infused in us from outside; we definitely possess them <within ourselves>".[157] In other words, morality and compassion are rooted in human nature.

But morality does not consist only in having certain rules of conduct. It also includes the ability to apply them appropriately in the varying circumstances we face. This requires moral *judgment*. And this too is available to all; one does not have to be an outstanding individual to have it. Unfortunately, many of us lose much of our capacity for moral reasoning through bad upbringing and bad education.

All humans are born with the capacity for moral judgment, the ability to think morally. This is part of most people's definition of what it is to be human. Courage means precisely knowing when to risk oneself; "courage to dare kills, courage not to dare saves" (Daodejing 73). Moderation means knowing how much you should have. Modern philosophers have only recently returned to the idea that character and virtue are an essential part of morality: they call this 'virtue ethics'. Exercising judgment is part of character; practical wisdom (*prudentia, phronesis*) is a moral virtue just as much as courage or moderation.

Morality is an attitude, an approach as much as it is a set of rules. Our conscience is our rudder in life. But it is not something that just speaks to us out of the blue (though it may do occasionally); rather, it is the capacity to decide and to decide well, "to respond well to one's circumstances". In order to apply rules, one has to use one's moral judgment all the time. In most situations, we have to weigh a whole set of possible outcomes and other factors all at once and pretty quickly. A lot of moral judgment relies on instinct, habit, character formation. "Each person has a... responsibility for identifying what counts as success in his own life".[158]

But none of this, and no moralist-- neither Confucius nor Mozi, neither Cicero nor Jesus-- confronts the brute facts which lie behind human self-interest or economic rationality (one sometimes wonders whether they were fully aware of them). This was Machiavelli's bombshell. The problem is that, when the other person is being driven by greed, lust or hate, it is completely contrary to our interests to treat them as we would treat those who are well-disposed to us. We have, therefore, no obvious duty to reciprocate or indeed to sympathise (though we may recognise that we are often so driven, so we should not write that off altogether). We have to treat them as calculating machines--play politics with them, defend ourselves, resist force with force.

The point then is, not that we ought to extend reciprocity to all humans regardless of their attitude or feelings towards us; but rather that these are the *only* relevant considerations. If the other person is willing to reciprocate and see the world from our point of view as well, then it doesn't matter whether that other mind is related to us or even personally known to us, whether (s)he belongs to the same state, nation or religion or has any other connection with us. But there can only be a universal community of people who are willing to engage in moral rationality.

We know that there are some people who are willing to reciprocate and take account of our viewpoint in every human group, in every state, religion and so on. We ought, therefore, to be willing to enter into alliance with, to work together with, all other groups of humans. How we do this depends on a multiplicity of factors in the everyday world. The rest is politics.

But what if others are not driven by greed and so on, yet still contest our reasonable wish to have enough to feed our own families, not out of hate, but quite simply because there is not enough food to go round everybody? Shoouldn't we try to get what *we* need?

Jesus' solution was that we should always give way to others ("love your enemies..."). Confucius rejected that option. Jesus' option may work in some close-knit personal relationships. It clearly does not work if you have a family to feed and someone else is trying to take what you have. (Jesus had no dependent family and believed that god was soon going to bring a favourable denouement to the human story anyway.)

You can either fight over it, or share what little there is between you. In that way, you have peace. These seem to be the only alternatives.

Morality and Knowledge

We have seen that moral conduct is partly based upon the ability to see another person's point of view. By promoting our understanding of other people, compassion goes hand in hand with our capacity to understand the world. The Daodejing put it the other way round: "mind opening leads to compassion" (DDJ 16). The ability to comprehend another's point of view, however, also improves our ability to compete with rivals; it is a factor in both love and strife. In either mode, this interaction with other beings who are of similar complexity to ourselves, seems to have been the context in which our faculty for calculation and reasoning developed.

We may also, however, suspect that in one way there is a closer connection between morality and human knowledge, that the development of these two peuliarly human characteristics is part of a single process.

If you care about someone else, you want to know what is in their mind, what may be troubling them. The kindest thing to say to someone who is ill or sad, is "What's wrong with you?" (an empirical question). In other words, compassion is empirical. Both compassion and science aim to tease out what the problem really is; both care passionately about detail. So compassion may be said to be part of human nature. (Darwin's theory of evolution was partly inspired by his empathy with living things.) Moral virtue and intellectual enquiry develop together.

Seeing anything clearly requires accurate and painstaking observation and calculation; one has to observe truthfully (be honest with oneself about) whatever one is seeing or experiencing. This is especially true in scientific investigation.

Being humane depends upon an understanding of other people, and at the same time it develops our understanding of others. Our ability to think, and calculate the consequences of our actions, enables us to submit gut instincts to examination. To do so is part of being human. It is not human always to act on gut instincts unfiltered and unconsidered. Confucius in particular made the connection between morality and knowledge perfectly clear. He defined humaneness as "love your fellow men", wisdom as "know your fellow men" (12:22). Doing one's best involves "using oneself to gauge others" (Analects 4:15).

Education

In order to induce good behaviour in the large and complex societies in which nearly all of us live nowadays, especially among strangers and across borders, we need both moral argument and education. Everyone knows that people's moral values depend to an alarming extent on the way they have been brought up. Education and philosophy both build on our evolved instincts for "good" behaviour, but they also have to counteract the equally strong instincts of hatred for outsiders and amoral competition.

Education equips us to understand the world by methods not otherwise available to humans (logic, science, mathematics and philosophy). The most important part of education is not teaching facts but how to acquire and make sense of facts. Logic, science, mathematics and languages are much more important than history, geography or sociology. Give a child these, and they are equipped for life, for decision-making and facing the conundrum of new problems. And again, everyone should be taught manual skills, how to put up shelves, grow vegetables, or build a wall.

Education can develop attitudes and behaviour which enable individuals to live well together, for their own sake and for their companions. It trains us to behave in a productive and comradely way not so much explicitly, as one teaches facts or a method of analysis, but obliquely, through story-telling, poetry and the teacher's personality.

The heart as well as the mind needs education. Singing, dancing, sport are as important as science and technical subjects. Hiking and camping together develop the ability to work as a team and a sense of wonder at the natural world. Voluntary social work is the crown of moral education.

The economic rationality which drives competition between individuals and which has done so much to create our present way of life in the global economy, has to be combined with *moral rationality*. In the long run, we may only be able to function adequately--only, perhaps, survive--if we take into account the interests of *all* other human beings. The two can be combined: it is in our best interests to be moral. There is no contradiction here: all we are doing is recognising that nowadays the fundamental interest of every individual--survival--requires a commmon pursuit of the interests of every other individual. Humanity has a manifest identity of interests. Competition works, but only within rules which are partly determined by morality. But without moral rationality we will all perish.

We have to realise that it is in our interests to treat others as we would ourselves, not only within the family and among friends but the world over. We have to develop reciprocity and empathy in our dealings with the widest community of all: humanity as a whole.

A World Community

This, then, is a basis for a world community, and some form of world state. Achieving a world state will be much easier if we have some kind of fellow-feeling for other human beings in different parts of the world, like that which is generated by national or religious identity. The most successful larger groups so far are in fact nation-states and religious communities. The fact that we have been able to develop a sense of citizenship in large groups such as nations and states suggests that a further development to a world state is, at least, not impossible. This would also help us to recognise the need for legitimate international coercion.

It will help if we have some way of picturing to ourselves humanity as a whole, and it will help even more if we have some form of organization which extends over the whole species. There are several partial world communities already in existence. Some kind of international community has already been achieved by Christians and Muslims. Such world religions draw together people of different backgrounds and races through beliefs and feelings which they all share. True, these exclude non-believers. But at least they suggest that people can feel united with one another on a global scale, insofar as they hold the same things dear. Then there is the worldwide scientific community with a common language.

Religion as we know to our cost is not enough, because people adhere to several different faiths, and in most of its present-day manifestations believers exclude outsiders from any kind of communal bond.

The problem is that both nations and religions tend to ground their cohesion upon perception of a common enemy. This applies in particular to western-style nation-states and to many current versions of Islam. Let us just hope that the absence of a common enemy does not mean that a community of all humans is impossible.

Jesus' strategy of always forgiving the faults of others works only if the aggressor is prepared to change their future behaviour. In other words, it emphasises only one side of the tit-for-tat equation. A general disposition to forgiveness is, however, extremely helpful, indeed essential, if we are to achieve harmony between different faith (or non-faith) groups, as is sadly demonstrated in the Middle East today. We are after all threatened by a common enemy (an impersonal one): climate change. When the species itself is under threat, it would be useful if we had within us some mental and moral stimulus driving us into wider sympathies for the whole species.

The ability to reason is the result of natural selection. But just as, once it appeared, it had applications far beyond the kinds of problems it was evolved to solve (in nuclear physics, for example), so rationality has a role in aspects of human conduct, for example international relations, to which it has only very recently begun to be applied.

The logic of a worldwide society of all men and women is that it can be based on what we all share, that is, on what makes us human: reason and the moral sense. Our ability to reason and investigate, which enables us to do science and philosophy, is shared by all human beings. This should make it possible for there to be a single community of all humans (*cosmopolis*).[159] Our mental abilities are, alas, leading us to do things that are catastrophic for our species: climate change is a result of human cleverness and scientific know-how. So we urgently need to use our capacity for moral understanding, which (as we have seen) arises partly out of our social brain, to counteract the effects of the rationality which arises out of our technological brain-- if we are to survive.

We share with all our fellow-humans an overriding common interest in keeping our planet habitable. For either it will be habitable for everyone, or for no-one. Climate change will not affect only the Inuit and Pacific islanders; it will have a huge impact on all of us.

The situation we are in presents us with a new kind of moral challenge. It means that we have to take account of future generations as never before. We have to ask ourselves how our actions are going to affect future generations--the unborn, our own descendants and everyone else's. We know, as we have never known before, how much what we do will affect future generations, they have to be considered just as much as those around us.

I sit here, drinking wine and watching the sun go down, while millions of children are under-nourished. This is a terrible fact. It is not my fault exactly. But what can I do about it?

The human species cannot flourish, even perhaps survive, without cooperation among all its members. Conflict within the species no longer serves any purpose because of its potential to inflict yet greater wounds on everyone, whether through nuclear or biological war, or by speeding up-- or neglecting-- the processes behind climate change.

All human societies, not least nation-states and religious communities, tend to regard their own norms as absolute. This creates obvious problems whenever different moral cultures come into contact, as they almost invariably do today, and increasingly so.

This problem can only be solved by something like human rights, the idea that certain ways of acting are moral, and other ways immoral, regardless of the backgrounds of the persons involved. In other words, certain basic or minimal duties and rights which everyone must observe in their relations with others: the rights to life, liberty and property express the duty not to kill, steal, rape. This assumes that it is reasonable to apply moral principles not only to members of one's own society or culture, but to all humans, precisely because they all have the same kind of mind as our own. If we base reciprocity on our ability to see inside other people's minds (as a precondition for understanding our own), then it must apply to all those with minds like our own, which means all humans.

This was what Stoic and Christian thinkers meant when they spoke of duties, such as respect for the life and property of others, as being a "law of nature". Rules about other people's lives and property are found in every human society. Indeed, "no-one knows where they came from" (as Sophecles put it). Winston Churchill put it this way, shortly before he led Britain to war against the Nazis: "One rule of conduct alone survives as a guide to men in their wanderings: fidelity to covenants, the honour of soldiers, and the hatred of causing human woe". [160]

Today, such ideas form the basis of international law. Implementing them in practice is the most difficult task conceivable. Establishing an agreed definition of, for example, property rights, and settling on agreed methods for safeguarding these and punishing defaulters, requires not just some kind of reasoned argument but phenomenal political skill. But, if we are to achieve peace and work together in the world of today, we have to have a measure of agreement about what is right and wrong.

In this way reciprocity and empathy are universalised. We have seen how these can be made--or, more precisely, just are--applicable not only to your kin group or those you come into regular contact with, nor even (as in a state, for example) to those with whom you are likely to come into contact, but to all human beings just because they are what they are. This is because all other humans have the same mental capacities as ourselves: there are certain things which they do not wish to be done to them any more than we do: murder, rape, theft.

Happiness

Another way of looking at the relationship between morality and competitive rationality is to ask what it is that makes us humans happy. What brings us to fulfilment as the sort of beings we are in the world? Is there a connection between morality and happiness?

According to the Dalai Lama, 'the very purpose of our life is to seek happiness'.[161] I think not. Humans are driven by forces of evolution and culture, and by the endless variety of whims of individuals. But this is hardly the same as saying we pursue happiness as a goal for its own sake. I doubt if many people have an idea of what 'happiness' as an abstract something is.

Among the forces driving us we may distinguish appetite, imagination and calculation (reason). Our physical appetite is for most of us most of the time the strongest motive in our lives. If you look around any supermarket, for example, you could be forgiven for thinking humans are stomachs with brains--instructions on how to fill them, also called the soul--attached. Eating comes first, then preaching, as Brecht put it in *The Threepenny Opera*.

The satisfaction of our appetites gives us pleasure, so we keep on doing it. We derive pleasure from using (interesting word) our imagination, whether to conjure up a pretty body or a gripping tale. And we use the power of calculation or reason to ensure that we succeed in satisfying our appetites, and attaining the desirable objects presented to us by our imagination.

Happiness is something more long-term, a sense of contentment and perhaps coupled with exhilaration, acquired through the satisfaction of appetite and imagination plus some confidence that we are going to be able to go on satisfying these.

So people probably don't make happiness their goal in life. To do so might be a category mistake, like looking for love. Yes, everyone wants to be happy, but you don't become happy by trying to be happy. It can't be planned any more than you can plan to fall in love. You may find it but not seek it (*pace* Jesus, who rather absurdly--I believed him once--said, "seek and you shall find").

Being happy is trendy, chic. The Dalai Lama looks happy. Perhaps I am not the right person to write about this since I don't feel happy much of the time. Most people who write about happiness give the impression (deliberately or otherwise) that they are indeed happy. Perhaps this is regarded as a necessary qualification for writing about it ("I've made it. And here's how"). Are such people blissfully unaware that one day they may be unhappy? "Call no-one happy till they're dead", as Solon said to king Croesus at the height of his wealth and power; Croesus was eventually defeated by a rival and tortured to death. If you sit back and say, "I'm happy", something is probably just about to go nastily wrong. And our minds are always prowling around looking for something new, something interesting we haven't yet had, which will probably disturb our peace of mind if we have any.

The happy person may be unaware that (s)he is happy. Part of the secret of happiness is a retreat from the kind of self-consciousness where you think about yourself to the point of bothering whether you are happy or not.

Happiness can come when you least expect it. It is a side-effect of what you do and the way you are. You breathe it but can't touch it. It hovers around you, creeps up on you, evaporates. Like "meaning", it slips past in the interstices of the mind. It comes and it goes. Wait for the next day.

What is "happiness" and how do we get there? It is widely believed that it consists in having plenty of money, a nice house, and going on vacations to exotic places-- and of course having a beautiful partner. According to recent research, a better standard of living increases a person's happiness, but only up to a certain point. Water, food, shelter are essential. But you don't need more than a certain amount of these to be happy.[162] Beyond that, material goods don't count for much. This is not to say that people who do have enough of these things are necessarily happy; but it is very difficult indeed to be happy without them. The same is true of physical health. As you approach death, material circumstances presumably count for much less.

It is said that genes account for roughly half our predisposition to be happy or unhappy.[163] Upbringing also counts for a lot. There again, a "good" upbringing does not necessarily make you happy, or guarantee fulfilment later in life. One knows of disastrous individuals from lovely homes. Both our genetic makeup and our upbringing are entirely outside our control.

One may distinguish between the temporary 'high' (euphoria) and inner contentment or fulfilment. But the two are connected. You can get euphoria from having a good meal, being in good company, or even getting drunk; but only if you were reasonably content to start with. "What is this intoxicating potion which intoxicates you and yet clarifies the mind, sets you at ease with yourself and enables you to perceive the ultimate truths about life?"[164]

People find fulfilment and inner contentment, and also euphoria, in widely different things. When Achilles, the hero of ancient Greek mythology, was born, his mother was told he could have one of two fates: he could return home and live to a ripe old age, or die at Troy and his name would last for ever. He could not choose both. Many would rather have a great adventure or achievement than lifelong peace of mind; in many cases it seems you can't have both. Obviously, which one prefers (no-one is given a choice in these matters) defines one's view of what makes life worth living.

Some are seduced by the idea of a fixed path. There are many misleading maps. Religions, such as Christianity, Buddhism or Islam are somewhat deceptive when they promise happiness to anyone who will live their life in a certain way. Plato said we progress from pleasures of the body to pleasures of the mind, a road map which influenced Christianity; the monastic way of life was seen as a kind of climax. Big mistake, probably.

Everyone needs some guidance, some signposts, but not too much or too many. We have to measure what others tell us against our own internal compass. At some point we have to figure out our own path. Everyone has the right to be happy in their own way (as Frederick the Great of Prussia once said).

People experience "moments of happiness", when they hear their children burst out laughing, or suddenly discover something. Different people find euphoria in different things. Some people are happy playing the guitar, others are happy rock-climbing. You get a different kind of satisfaction from a pay rise, and even more from getting a job you were after; still more, from having your achievements recognised. The most intense euphoria is being in love.

But of course all of these sensations and experiences can be reversed (as we know only too well). The things we enjoy most don't last long. There again, we may think happiness is things staying as they are for as long as possible; or we may be looking for new sources of excitement. But in some ways happiness and unhappiness accumulate over a lifetime.

Being Good and Being Happy

Happiness is geared to other people. No man or woman can be exist without other people. As being good means behaving towards other people in the same way that we wish them to behave towards us, so our personal well-being, our euphoria and our inner happiness depend a lot on how we get on with other people. People who are badly off but have good relationships are generally happier than people who are rich but lonely.[165]

There is, then, a strong and vital connection between morality and happiness. The ultimate cure for depression, for feelings of worthlessness, for the feeling that "life is not worth living", is to live for others (as

Beethoven discsovered).[166] So long as the be-all and end-all of your life is your own satisfaction, you will always be disappointed.

Relationships

And just as the foundations of moral virtue--reciprocity and empathy--exist in the most intimate relationships of family and friendship--between woman and man, child and parent--so the foundations of satisfaction in life exist there too. The same is true of friends. No-one can be happy without friends--people with whom one can share thoughts. Friends help one another through times of stress. Friends are, generally speaking, for life: you would not consider someone a friend if you didn't think the relationship was, so far as you could tell at the time, a permanent one. Just as reciprocity and empathy evolved in the small groups of family and friends or comrades, so our happiness develops there too.

We can have meaningful relationships with the people we work with (or some of them), or with people we meet for recreation and fun, or with neighbours. And we have particular moral responsibilities towards these wider communities; and we can also derive particular personal satisfaction and pleasure from them. These too can be a focus for reciprocity and empathy. Here again virtue and happiness go side by side. It is a pity that recent writings on virtue ethics have not recognised the communal aspect of the good life but seem to talk only of "individual flourishing".[167]

What about relationships with strangers? How else do you make new friends? And by helping someone else, chatting to someone on some random occasion, you can enjoy a sympathy of minds. This warms the heart more when it is unexpected (one reason for using public transport). We need public social spaces, places for chance meetings.

Vocation

Everyone can make a unique contribution to society in the way they relate to other people. Voluntary work-- hospital visiting, talking through disputes between neighbours and so on-- gives someone a vital role. As you get to know those who need someone to talk to, you may become irreplaceable. By helping others, you become important to them. You matter; others depend on you. So everyone has somewhere they can fit in.

Everyone needs to be valued by others. Whether or not others value someone depends of course largely on that person. To be happy, one needs the esteem of people who value you just for who you are. The Roman poet Virgil, in his description of paradise (Elysium) noted that there were not only of heroes present but people "who made others remember them for what they deserved" (*Aeneid* 6: 664). Social recognition ratchets up your self-esteem. (Fame refers to social recognition in a much larger group of people, and is probably a different story.) The greatest social esteem goes to those who commit themselves to a cause for the common good of society, or who sacrifice their safety for others. These satisfactions are open to everybody (even if they live in Waziristan). And everyone over the age of about 30 knows that not to have such esteem is a major source of unhappiness.

Happiness also depends upon what we do. The good life for each person is related to their occupation. Some find self-fulfilment in a specific vocation. Everyone has some specific work or skill they are good at, and which few others (perhaps no-one) can do so well.[168] Manual and technical skills, from carpentry to computing, can be every bit as important to society and rewarding to the individual as being a great scientist or an outstanding leader. Technical education is as important as education in science or the humanities. Everyone should have some grounding in manual skills, such as how to construct a wall. The sixth-century monk St Benedict introduced the praxis of manual labour as an intrinsic part of a good life and so probably encouraged the development of agriculture--a much underrated factor in 'the rise of the West'.

Practising a talent is hard work. But it is wonderful to have a skill which you alone can perform in that particular way, a task which you alone are equipped to fulfil, and which, if you were not around, would not get done, or not so well done. But if this is what society pays you to do, you are extremely lucky.

If you can't get paid employment in what you're good at, you can do it voluntarily. Nowadays, perhaps more than ever, a happy life (for a Westerner) depends on having satisfying leisure pursuits, things you enjoy doing even though you don't have to do them, and don't get paid for doing them. Even if you have to work eight hours a day at something you don't particularly like, you can still write poetry or run a club in the evenings. Everyone needs something which they can do well, through which they can gain recognition from others.

Happiness is not, however, dependent on expertise, mental or physical. Professional philosophers--people who practise the academic discipline which goes by that name today--have on average neither more nor less real practical knowledge about how to be happy than business executives or bin-men. Artists, scientists, inventors are not necessarily happy. Moments of intense inspiration may be followed by hours of introspective misery. Beethoven contemplated suicide; the man who created the computer, Alan Turing, did commit suicide. I suspect that few write poetry without having been through some ghastly experience.

Fulfilment: an Indian view

According to the Indian tradition, fufilment comes in four spheres of life which everyone needs to engage in at some point: virtue, sensual pleasure, political economy (eg. running a household), and inner well-being, spiritual peace.[169] Each has its own part to play in our lives; none should be allowed to obliterate others. Each should be given free play. One should not pursue truth or virtue to the exclusion of pleasure; nor lose inner well-being in the pursuit of money. In the Bhagavad-Gita, however, the god Krishna insists that the hero Arjuna must pursue his vocation as a warrior even though this means killing close relatives. This 'works' morally only because death is not the end and the chain of cause and effect will be worked out in future lives, just as one's present status derives from previous ones.

This contrasts with the Western way of looking at things, which tends to emphasise consistency. The danger is that one may miss the unique qualities of different things. Having a variety of goals may leave you more free to make your own judgment according to each situation. When the demands of different spheres clash, you surely have to work it out for yourself, without assuming that any one must take precedence.

Happiness and Human Nature

One argument, then, in favour of compassion and against antagonism, in favour of the moral as opposed to the competitive mode of rationality, lies in human nature itself: that is, in the feeling of fulfilment as a human being which moral conduct brings with it, and which mere competitive conduct does not: the feeling of self-worth that comes from doing what you know to be right. Here too lies a connection between morality and happiness. There seems to be a particularly strong relationship between acting rightly and feeling good (feeling yourself) as a human being. When someone does good to others, or works for the good of society as a whole, they can get the sense that what they are doing is what they were brought into existence to do.

This has been expressed in both Eastern and Western thought. It is what Confucius and others meant by "the noble person (*junzi*)"; his or her "true nature-- humaneness, justice, propriety and knowledge-- is rooted in his heart".[170] Such a one "cannot be subverted by power or profit, nor swayed by the masses... nor unsettled by the whole world... This is what is called holding firm to inner power. He who holds firm to inner power is able to order himself; being able to order himself, he can then respond to others" (Xunzi).[171] Or as the Roman poet Horace put it, "the just man who clings to his purpose will not be shaken from his firm spirit by eager citizens urging him to do wrong or by a tyrant's glowering looks" (*Odes* III.3).

The Mind and the Cosmos: The Joy of Thought

We find meaning in our families and friends, our work, culture, nature and art; in their beauty. It helps if one has a cosmic dimension to one's life. Belief in "god" may make someone happy, or it may not. Belief in a life after death may make someone happy, or it may not. But we need to relate in some way to nature and the cosmos. This usually develops over time. Parents and teachers may give us clues; or they may mislead us. Their most common fault is that they stop us looking.

Of all the things that make for happiness or unhappiness, for inner contentment or fulfilment, what people have most control over is their own mind and the choices they make. Whether a person is happy or unhappy depends on their whole outlook and their awareness of the world. The health, or good repair, of the mind is something which most of us do not pay much attention to, less attention perhaps than we pay to computers and holidays; unless something goes seriously wrong. Sometimes people pay too much attention to it.

On the face of it, our condition in a cosmos without "god" and with no prospect of life after death, is forlorn. "Unhappy human life! When things go well--like a shadow; when things go badly--a wet sponge wipes the picture out."[172]

What consolations are there? Self-awareness, eros, relationships with other people, the beauty and wonder of the universe. Facts, even unsavoury ones, taste good in the mind. Nothing is greater than the pleasure of thought.

We are not the first to be in this predicament. The cosmos was bleaker for the ancient Greeks and Romans than for Jews, Christians and Muslims. "Of all that breathes and crawls upon the earth, nothing is more miserable than man" (Homer, *Iliad* 17: 446). "The wet drink of the grape cluster... puts an end to the pain men suffer, whenever they are filled with the flow that comes from the vine, it gives them sleep to make them forget the ills besetting them day by day: there is no other drug against their suffering."[173]

We find among the Greeks and Romans a view of humanity and the cosmos to which we can relate better than people perhaps thought they could before modern scientific discoveries: there is no prospect of a happy afterlife, yet the world is a cause for wonder. "The good man... seeks happiness without talk of the hereafter."[174]

We do not need anti-depressants to find a basis within ourselves, solace in the face of reality. The writings of the Greeks and Romans still reach us; they provide a compass, a sympathetic understanding of what it is to be human, of the tremendous dimensions of our lives. Knowledge of all this has largely disappeared from Western culture at the very moment when we need it most. (Nowadays "Western civilization" means you can say what you want, but no-one reads Aeschylus-- whose poetry lifts and sways like a boat surging.) They may help us face the kind of universe we inhabit. "Remember the whole of existence; you are a tiny part of it".[175]

We need a way of being happy which goes along with what we know about the world we live in, with the way we know the world is. We are mental creatures, and for us being happy depends partly upon having an understanding of the world around us which enables us to come to terms with it. Our brains were evolved partly to find out what the world we live in is like; if we don't do this, our minds will be dissatisfied. So Marcus

Aurelius insisted that "the happiness of man lies in... contemplation of the nature of the universe".[176] The trouble is nost people don't realise this: "although reason (logos) is common to all, most live as though they had a private understanding".[177]

Personal fulfilment is reached by searching for truth, helping promote the common good of a society, looking at the beauties of the cosmos and appreciating them. These have roots in the evolution of the technological, social and natural-history aspects of the human brain.[178] But in humans these develop a whole series of new mental activities: music, mathematicss, science, religion, art. They can make us feel good. They develop a logic of their own beyond what started them off.

The genuine, honest person is a rare gem. To know such a person is a greater privilege than to know a great leader or an artistic genius. The Roman poet Virgil numbered among the blessed who live in the fields of Elysium those who made other remember them just by who they were. Or, as the Book of Ecclesiastes has it: 'And some there be which have no memorial; they are perished as if they had never been. But their name liveth for evermore'.

Fulfilment or inner contentment comes from finding your place in the world, your purpose; finding yourself, being happy with who you are, feeling whole--integrity. While euphoria tends to be up and down, fulfilment or lack of it tends to accumulate over a lifetime. Then again some mishap, death, or just old age might take that away (call no-one happy till they're dead).

Everyone, of course, has to learn to live with elements of uncertainty about what the world is like. If we *don't* know something, we have to learn to live with that, not invent answers that aren't there. If we invent answers, we end up in a state of tension between what we are trying to think and something inside us that knows this is not true (cognitive dissonance). This can make us unhappy and lead to mental problems.

We cannot be happy if we are confused or dishonest (there's justice for you). We avoid confusion and dishonesty by recognizing things as they are, accepting the world as it is, and trying to find out more about it. If one tries to use the mind to reconstruct reality the way you would like it to be--whether by refusing to acknowledge that something has happened, or that such-and-such is the case, or by re-living some past mistake, or by imagining things that have not happened or do not exist--one is asking for trouble. The mind can't do that; it thrashes around like a beached whale.

The search for meaning and understanding goes on, consciously or unconsciously, throughout one's life, whether one wants it or not. It can be resisted, but at a price. One may lose track of it, abandon it, avoid it. But it will come back to you (like any natural desire). This is one of the things which is most precious to the human mind (ask any scientist, artist, theologian or philosopher). It will unsettle you, give you hell, but without it your life is neutered, just as it is without other kinds of desire such as eros. We continue to search for meaning and love until the moment we die.

Pain and Sadness

Suffering is part of nature. Pain is an evolved method of letting you know there is something wrong and warning you to take action. In that sense, it has a purpose. The same is true of mental pain. Presumably humans experience this in a more acute form than any other animal because of their bigger and more complex brains.

Sadness is the natural, appropriate reaction to the adversities we all experience in some form or another. It is neither natural nor appropriate to be happy all the time. Someone who was would be insensitive and possibly deranged. Unhappiness may come from our failure to get something we had set our heart on, our failure to achieve some deeply desired goal, or from the death of a loved one, or even alienation from them. It may be the result of defeat in war. Animals feel sadness. Occasional sadness is a recognition of our very real limitations, as individuals, as communities, and as a species. So the ultimate good for the human soul is not so much happiness as sanity.

To be sad in this way doesn't merely alert the mind to a problem. We could see the problem without feeling sad about it. But it may put us in touch with a deeper reality, one which we would not be aware of without feeling sad sometimes: the presence of those awful facts in our lives, in the cosmos. In this way, we may afterwards learn something worth learning. There is nothing wrong with being sad. If you can accept sadness, you can be happy.

The Greek poet Aeschylus identified the supreme deity as "the one who set humans on the path to wisdom, made 'learn through suffering' the sovereign rule"; pain "drips through sleep and onto the heart; and even those who did not want to, become wise" (Agamemnon lines 176-81). Buddhism explains the use of adversity by saying that, whereas the unskilled farmer throws away his shit, the skilled farmer uses it to manure his fields. A Christian writer said that God teaches the heart not by ideas but by pains and contradictions.

One explanation comes from ancient China. "When Heaven intends to confer on a person great responsibility it first visits his mind with suffering, toils his sinews and bones, subjects his body to hunger, exposes him to poverty, and confounds his projects. Through this, his mind is stimulated, his nature strengthened, and his inadequacies repaired. People... are able to reform; their minds are troubled and their thoughts perplexed, but then they become capable of acting".[179] Again, "If you do not climb a high mountain, you will not know the height of Heaven; if you do not look down into a deep valley, you will not know the depths of the earth... If there is no dark and dogged will, there will be no bright and shining clarity; if there is no dull and determined effort, there will be no brilliant and glorious achievement".[180]

Depression is something else. In our society, mental illness has, for a whole variety of reasons, become an epidemic; and we seem to know as little about how to deal with it as our ancestors knew about bacterial infection. The mind exists to alert you to problems; and, if it spots a problem, it won't let you go until you have paid attention to it. Otherwise it becomes restless, disorientated, anxious, locked into pointless thoughts (perhaps quite nasty ones).

When we are depressed, it looks as if there is no way out, and no reason to think that one's mind or circumstances are ever going to change. But it is an absolute truth--indeed, a law of nature--that, however depressed we may feel, circumstances will change, something new will happen. Whatever you see at the present is only part of the picture. *Either* (1) circumstances are not so bad as you think they are, *or* (2) they are, in some way or another, different from what you think they are; *or* (3) they will change. No state of mind, no set of circumstances stays the same for long. Yesterday's pain is part of today's landscape.

Relax

Relaxation is as necessary to the mind as sleep to the body. The mind, like any other organ or muscle, needs both exercise and relaxation.

Just because we are born with various body parts doesn't mean we know how to use them in all the situations we get into. We don't need to be taught how to defecate or swallow, but we do need to be taught how to produce vegetables and build cupboards. Since the brain is the most complicated part of us, it may not be surprising if we don't start off knowing everything about it, about how to use it and how best to look after it.

Ways of relaxing and healing the mind and maintaining its health were developed in Eastern cultures, while the West was busy developing science and technology. Yoga and Tai chi are two examples. But the fruits of these cultures can now be be used by everybody.

Rituals are one way of relaxing the mind, taking oneself outside the stream of one's immediate discourse. The method of rituals is to make one do things which have no obvious purpose (dancing, music).

People have different ways of relaxing their minds. You can focus on any object-- a flower or a door-knob-- and, whenever you find your mind has wandered onto something else, bring it gently back to that point. You can focus on breathing. Three minutes is a long time. As with physical exercise, the effects don't show up for a while.

Through focussing your mind in this way, you even forget yourself and begin to find oneness with life, with matter-and-energy. Perhaps you can apply relativity to yourself. One may find oneself in a state of semi-non-consciousness; you are aware, but not of anything in particular. Very gradually, a sense of something other than one's own circumstances and one's own consciousness, dawns on one. There is nothing emotional, nothing exciting, nothing uplifting, just calm, empty, still water; like a theory that works.

Meditation enables you to find within yourself a place set apart, a inner space of still delight, where our interests and ideas no longer apply. It does actually helps you to sleep as well. The joy of consciousness is part of being an entity with such a large and complex brain. Everyone needs meditation. Everyone can have it. Unfortunately, it seems to be one of the best kept secrets on the planet. Maybe people just don't think they need it. Big mistake.

Given the size of the universe, it is just possible that life exists, has existed, or will exist somewhere else in the universe.[181] Some think the evolutionary advantages of consciousness and intelligence make it likely that other intelligent beings have evolved, are evolving, or will evolve, elsewhere in the cosmos. Given the distances in space and time, it is highly unlikely that we will ever come into contact with them, if they are there, or they with us.

If there are other intelligent beings, and if their intelligence has, like ours, evolved through social interaction, they too would surely develop morality. It is conceivable that their morality would, like ours, be based on reciprocity and compassion. The same norms of honest thought and honest dealing might hold good for them as for us.

Our thoughts, our system of being, our philosophy, our acts of honour may have taken place among other beings in other systems, and may take place again. They *could* be as universal as the laws of physics. Human activities, such as science, art, helping others, will be as noble and honourable at the end of our time as they were at the beginning. It will be just as noble to be doing these things then, however daunting the prospect facing us all, as it ever was.

The stirrings, strivings, discoveries of our minds may be shared by others in other parts of the cosmos. They too may acquire (limited) knowledge about the structure of the universe, about fundamental particles and so on, like us. And they too, like us, might engineer their own destruction

Epilogue

The stones, washed this way and that by sea and stream, shaped by ice and wind, were here long before we were and will be here long after we have gone. In the highland streams there are lots and lots of red and green stones of all shapes, sizes and hues. When the sun shines, the light catches them through the water and makes them many different shades of red and green.

One day a little girl came by and saw the stones: green, blue, faun, crimson, black. The colours of ancient explosions. She picked one up, cupped it in her hands, looked it over and said, "You're gorgeous". This was the only time anyone noticed.

Endnotes

1   The Economist 31st May 2014, p.49.

2   Martin Rees, *Our cosmic habitat* (London: Phoenix, 2003).

3   Particles produced by nuclear reactions within the sun.

4   Joseph Silk, *The infinite cosmos: questions from the frontiers of cosmology* (Oxford University Press, 2006): 185

5   J.B.S.Haldane, c.1900, quoted in John D. Barrow, *Impossibility: the limits of science and the science of limits* (Oxford University Press, 1998), p.99.

6   Richard Feynman, *Six easy pieces* (Princeton University Press, 1963), p. 136.

7   Craig Callendar, 'Is time an illusion?: Scientific American, June 2010:43.

8   Rees, *Cosmic Habitat*, pp. 59,92.

9   'When the distance scales involved are around the Planck length (a millionth of a billionth of a billionth of a billionth of a centimetre) or less, quantum mechanics invalidates the equations of general relativity': Brian Greene, *The elegant universe: superstrings, hidden dimensions, and the quest for the ultimate theory* (London: Jonathan Cape, 1999): 235, 130.

10   John D. Barrow, *Theories of everything: the quest for ultimate explanation* (Oxford University Press, 1990); Rees, Cosmic Habitat, p. 153; Greene, Elegant Universe, p. 385.

11 Barrow, *Impossibility*, pp. 209, 218, 250.

12 Rees, *Cosmic Habitat*, p. 63

13 Pritchard, James B., ed., *Ancient Near Eastern Texts relating to the Old Testament* (Princeton, NJ: Princeton University Press, 1955), pp. 405-7.

14 Plato, *Apology* 31D

15 *The Guardian* 9.8.08 Saturday Review p. 11.

16 The medieval philosopher Duns Scotus built *a whole theory of knowledge and being around this*.

17 *Life and Fate*, trans. Robert Chandler (Penguin 1990), p. 555.

18 Edward O. Wilson, *Consilience; the unity of knowledge* (New York: Knopf, 1998): 107, 109-10, 135.

19 Nicholas Gaiano in *Scientific American* July 2012 p.3

20 Trans. Arthur Waley (New York; Grove Press, 1996); also known as *The Classic of Odes, mostly dating from the early first millenium BCE.*

21 Ezra Pound, 'Erat hora', lines 4-8.

22 Pindar, cit. Christian Meier, *The Greek discovery of politics,* trans. David McLintock (Cambridge Mass: Harvard University Press, 1990), p.45

23 Edward A. Westermarck, (1890), *The History of Human Marriage.*

24 Steven Pinker, *The Language Instinct: the new science of language and mind* (London, Penguin, 1994).

25 Lumsden Charles J. and Wilson, Edward O., *Genes, Mind and Culture: the Co-evolutionary Process*, Cambridge MA, Harvard University Press, 1981

26 Alison Gopnik, 'How babies think': *Scientific American* July 2010: 59-60. Children's brains 'unconsciously (process) information in a way that parallels the methods of scientific discovery'.

27 *Autobiography* (2003) pp. 150, 176.

28 *The Economist*, 28th. April 2012.

29 Wilson, *Consilience*, pp. 55, 85-6.

30 *Robert Trivers has recently suggested that economics should be reconstructed on the foundation of evolutionary biology: Deceit and self-deception* (Allen Lane, 2011).

31 Popper, Karl R. (1957), *The Poverty of Historicism, London, Routledge and Kegan Paul,* 1957.

32 Oxford University Press, 2008.

33 *Guild and State: European Political Thought from the Twelfth Century to the Present* (Transaction Books, 2003).

34 Isaac Deutscher, *The Prophet Outcast* (Oxford Unicersity Press, 1963).

35 Karl Popper, *Unended Quest: an intellectual autobiography* (Glasgow: Collins, 1976)

36 . *The Oxford History of Ancient Egypt*, ed. Ian Shaw, (Oxford: Oxford University Press, 2000).

37 Karl Jaspers, 'The axial period', in his *The origin and goal of human history* (New Haven NJ: Yale University Press 1947):1-25.

38 Holmes, Richard, *The Age of Wonder: how the Romantic generation discovered the beauty and terror of science,* London, HarperCollins, 2008.

39 Assmann, Jan, *The Search for God in Ancient Egypt* (Ithaca, New York: Cornell University Press, 2001), p. 187.

40 Aeschylus, *Agamemnon*, lines 160-6.

41 www.edge.org/3rd_culture/heisenberg07.

42 *The Bhagavad Gita*, trans. Juan Mascaro (Penguin, 1962), pp. 49-50.

43 Alain de Botton, *Religion for Atheists: a non-believer's guide to the uses of religion* (Hamish Hamilton 2012).

44 Dodds, E.R. (1951), *The Greeks and the Irrational* (Berkeley CA: University of California Press). p. 29.

45 Putnam, Robert (2000), *Bowling Alone: the collapse and revival of American community* (New York, Simon and Schuster, 2000).

46 Rappaport, Roy A., *Ritual and Religion in the making of humanity* (Cambridge: Cambridge University Press, 1999)

47   Assmann, Jan, *The Search for God in Ancient Egypt*, trans. D.Lorton (Ithaca NY: Cornell University Press, 2001).

48   Kulke, Hermann and Rothermund, Dietmar, *History of India*, 3rd edn (London, Routledge, 1998), pp. 184-223.

49   Kate Armstrong, *The Case for God: what religion really means* (London: The Bodley Head, 2009), p. 4.

50   Rowan Williams (2008), *Dostoevsky: language, faith and fiction* (London, Continuum, 2008). We need 'a human value that can only be grounded in God' (p. 235).

51   See Durkheim, Emile, *The Elementary Forms of Religious Life,* trans. Karen Fields (New York, The Free Press 1995/ 1912).

52   Terry Eagleton, *Reason, Faith and Revolution: reflection's on the God debate* (Yale University Press, 2009).

53   Israel Shahak, *Jewish History, Jewish Religion: the weight of three thousand years,* (London, Pluto, 1994).

54   Robert Fine, *Cosmopolitanism*, London, Routledge, 2007.

55   See Jennifer Welchman, *The Practice of Virtue: Classic and Contemporary Readings in Virtue Ethics* (Indianapolis IN: Hackett, 2006).

56   Armstrong, *The Case for God.*

57   Richard Dawkins, *The God Delusion* (London: Bantam, 2006).

58   For a recent survey, see *The Scientific American, The evolution of evolution: how Darwin's theory survives, thrives and reshapes the world* (special issue, Jan 2009).

59   See Baxter, Brian, *A Darwinian Worldview: sociology, environmental ethics and the work of Edward O. Wilson* (Aldershot, Ashgate, 2007), pp. 146-50.

60   On non-Abrahamic religions Dawkins merely says 'I shall not be concerned with other religions such as Buddhism or Confucianism' (*God Delusion*, p. 59), thus completely ignoring Hinduism, Daoism and so on.

61 Kirk, G.S., Raven, J.E., Schofield,M., *The Presocratic philosophers* (Cambridge University Press, 1983), 193.

62 'The whole created universe groans in all its parts': St. Paul, *Epistle to the Romans* 8:22. He had reason to know.

63 Greene, *Elegant Universe*, pp. 82-3, 235.

64 Silk, *Infinite Cosmos*, p. 184.

65 Barrow, *Impossibility*, p. 189; see also Bojowald in The *Scientific American* August 2008: 28-33.

66 Rees, *Cosmic Habitat*, pp. 71, 73.

67 Rees *Ibid.*, p. 158; Silk, *Infinite Cosmos*, p. 178; Greene, *Elegant Universe*, pp. 366-8.

68 Silk, *Infinite Cosmos*, p. 174.

69 Rees, *Cosmic Habitat*, p. 170; *Scientific American* Sept 2009:22-9.

70 Rees, *Cosmic Habitat*, p. 164

71 Greene, *Elegant Universe*, p. 368

72 This was already the view of Aristotle, followed by the Muslim philosopher Ibn Rushd (1126-98); Thomas Aquinas thought the immortality of the soul could only be known by divine revelation.

73 Gerard Manley Hopkins, 'God's Grandeur', line 10.

74 Martin Buber, *I and Thou* (Continuum, 2004)

75 http://edge.org/conversations/science-and-religion

76 According to Pauli, 'Einstein has a feeling for the central order of things. He can detect it in the simplicity of natural laws.'

77 Quoted by Silk, *Infinite Cosmos*, p. 218.

78 Silk, *ibid.*, pp. 155, 221, 225.

79 Tractatus logico-philosophicus, section 7: 'wovon man nicht sprechen kann, daruber muss man schweigen'.

80 Trans. J. Hopkins (Minneapolis, MN: Banning, 1985). See *The Cambridge History of Medieval Philosophy*, ed. R. Pasnau (Cambridge University Press, 2010), pp.725-6.

81 German folk song: 'Himmel und Erde sie mussen vergehen, allein die Musiker werden bestehen'.

82 *Sic et non*, eds Boyer and Mckeon, p.103.

83 Feynman *Six Pieces*, p. 60.

84 Notably in *De rerum natura* iv. 254ff.

85 Holmes, *Age of Wonder*.

86 *The Selected Poems of Li Po*, trans. David Hinton (London: Anvil Press, 1996), p.8.

87 Tahar ben Jelloun This Blinding Absence of Light, p. 127.

88 Vassily Grossman, *Life and Fate*, p.555

89 Wilson, *Sociobiology*, p.298-9

90 David Archer and Raymond Pierrehumbert, *The Warming Papers: the scientific foundation for climate change forecast* (Wiley: Blackwell,2011, p. 234.

91 *The Economist* 5th Dec 2009, special report, p.3); Robert Henson, (Penguin, 2006), *The Rough Guide to Climate Change*), p. 3; *Scientific American*, July 2011.

92 James Hansen, (2009), *Storms of My Grandchildren: the truth about the coming climate catastrophe and our last chance to save humanity* (London, Bloomsbury):76, 164.

93 *Rough Guide*, p. 4, 264.

94 *The Economist* 5th Dec 2009, special report, p.11.

95 IPCC, *Climate Change* 2007: Working group I: *the physical science basis*,p. 5

96 *Time Magazine* 14 Dec 2009,p. 45.

97 April 19th 2014, p.77

98 *Climate in Peril: a popular guide to the latest IPCC reports* (UNEP 2009): pp. 4,24; *The Economist* 19th April 2014, p.77.

99 *The Economist* 19th April 2014, p.77 (my italics).

100 *Climate in Peril*, p.24

101 Hansen, *Storms*,p. 164

[102] Hansen, *Storms*, 24.

[103] *Scientific American* December 2009, pp. 46-51.

[104] *Rough Guide*,p. 201

[105] Hansen, *Storms,*149

[106] *Climate in Peril*, p.6.

[107] *Climate in Peril*, p.6.

[108] Michael E. Mann in *Scientific American*, March 2012 p.69

[109] Conference at Exeter University, reported in *The Guardian* 9th. Dec 1008.

[110] IPCC, 2009 *Climate Change*, p.6; *Rough Guide*, 228.

[111] *Climate in Peril*, p. 41

[112] Hansen, *Storms*, 172

[113] *Climate in Peril*, P 55

[114] *Ibid*, p. 40; IPCC, *Climate Change*, p. 3

[115] *Time Magazine* 14 Dec 2009: 40-4.

[116] Hansen, *Storms*: 165

[117] *The Economist* 22nd Feb 2014, p. 53.

[118] *The Economist* 14th March 2009:82.

[119] *The Economist* 22nd Feb 2014, p. 68.

[120] Hansen, *Storms*: 160; *Rough Guide* 83-5

[121] *The Economist* 17th. March 2012,p. 58.

[122] Lovelock, James (2006), *The Revenge of Gaia: why the earth is fighting back-- and how we can still save humanity* (London, Allen Lane)

[123] 'And when they ask you why we died, Tell them that our fathers lied': an epitaph on the First World War by Rudyard Kipling, apostle of the British Empire, whose son was killed in 1917.

[124] Hansen, *Storms*: 171.

[125] Hansen, *Storms*: see especially pp. 11,91,94,110,125.

[126] So Mark Bowen proceeded to write a book, *Censoring Science: inside the political attack on Dr. James Hansen and the truth of global warming'* (2008).

127   BBC survey reported on 7th Dec 2009.

128   *Rough Guide*, pp. 302-3.

129   See Hansen, *Storms*: 172-4, 194, 201-2. Robert Socolow and Stephen Pacala of Princeton University have suggested a number of specific measures which together would solve our problem ('seven wedges'): *Scientific American* Sept 2006: 28-35.

130   Chairman of the 2013 IPCC: *The Independent* 28th Sept 2013, p.6.

131   IPCC 2007, *Global Environment Outlook-1*, p. 3; *Climate in Peril*,p. 44.

132   *The Economist* 19th April 2014, p.77.

133   *Climate in Peril*, p. 45.

134   Garvey, James (2008), *The Ethics of Climate Change: right and wrong in a warming world* (London, Continuum); Ernest Partidge, 'Future Generations' in Jamieson, D., ed. (2001), *A Companion to Environmental Philosophy,* Oxford, Blackwell: 377-89; Henry Shue, 'Human rights, climate change and the trillionth ton' in Denis G. Arnold, *The Ethics of global climate change* (Cambridge University Press, 2011): 392-314.

135   Elizabeth Cripps, *Climate Change and Moral Agency* (Oxford University Press, 2013).

136   Zweig, Stefan (1943), *The World of Yesterday: an autobiography* London, Cassell.

137   Robert Trivers, *Social Evolution* (Menlo Park, Calif, 1985) p. 393.

138   Axelrod, Robert, *The Evolution of Co-operation* (New York: Basic Books, 1984); Trivers, *Social Evolution*, p. 392.

139   J.R.Krebs and N.B.Davies, eds, *Behavioural Ecology: an evolutionary approach, 2nd edn* (Oxford: Blackwell, 1984), pp.83-4.

140   Hamilton, W. D. (1964), `*The evolution of social behaviour*', Journal of Theoretical Biology 7: 1-52; Trivers, *Social Evolution*, pp. 126-8.

141   Mark Pagel, *Wired for culture: the natural history of human co-operation* (Allen Lane, 2011).

142 Antony Black, *State, Community and Human Desire: a Group-centred Account of Political Values* (London: Wheatsheaf, and New York: St. Martin's Press, 1988.

143 Jan Luiten van Zanden, *The Long Road to the Industrial Revolution: the European economy in a global perspective* (Brill, 2009).

144 Mithen, Steven, *The Prehistory of the Mind: a search for the origins of art, religion and science* (London: Thames and Hudson, 1996).

145 *Treatise of human nature, part III* concl; see also section ii *'Of Greatness of Mind'*.

146 Krebs and Davies, *Behavioural Ecology*, p. 389.

147 Rappaport, Roy A., *Ritual and Religion in the making of humanity*(Cambridge: Cambridge University Press, 1999), pp. 132, 323

148 Laland, Kevin N. and Brown, Gillian R., *Sense and Nonsense: evolutionary perspectives on human behaviour* (Oxford: OxfordUniversity Press, 2002), p. 169

149 Glenny, Misha, *McMafia: seriously organised crime*, London, Vintage, 2009.

150 *Sources of Chinese Tradition, vol.1: from Earliest Times to 1600*, compiled by Wm. Theodore de Bary and Irene Bloom, ColumbiaUniversity Press 1999, p.70.

151 *Mozi/ Mo Tzu, Basic Writings, trans. Burton Watson*, Columbia University Press 1967, pp. 16-7; Graham, A.C., *Disputers of the Tao: philosophical argument in ancient China* (La Salle, Ill: Open Court, 1989), pp. 18-19

152 *'the human being is born to be benevolent': Meditations*, 3.4, 8.26, 9.5. Marcus was a Roman emperor committed to the pursuit of wisdom (philosophy).

153 In Grimsley, Ronald, *The Philosophy of Rousseau*, Oxford, Oxford University Press, 1973, p. 103.

[154] An Enquiry concerning the Principles of Morals, ch.2: *'Of Benevolence'* (my ital)

[155] *Meditations* 6:24, 9:28; 10.7.2; 11.20.1.

[156] Brown, Donald E., *Human Universals* (Philadelphia,PA: Temple University Press, 1991)

[157] Yuri Pines, *'Disputers of the Li:Breakthroughs in the concept of Ritual in pre-imperial China': Asia Major, 3rd series,* 13/1 (2000a): 28

[158] Ronald Dworkin, *Justice for Hedgehogs*, p.203

[159] Marcus Aurelius *Meditations*, 4.4

[160] Winston Churchill, *Marlborough, His life and times* (Harrap, 1947): vols 3-4,p. 993.

[161] H. H. Dalai Lama and Howard Cutler (1998), *The Art of Happiness: a handbook for living*, London, Hodder and Stoughton, p. 3.

[162] Layard, Richard (2005), *Happiness: lessons from a new science* (London, Allen Lane)

[163] *Scientific American* March 2007: 18, 22.

[164] Su Shi, *a Chinese poet* (1037-1101).

[165] Putnam, *Bowling Alone* (2000).

[166] *Heiligenstadt Testament*, October 6-10, 1802: Maynard Solomon, Beethoven (London: Granada, 1980: 170-3.

[167] See for example Christine Swanton, *Virtue Ethics: a pluralistic view* (Oxford University Press, 2003).

[168] *This idea of a person's specific 'vocation' to which each individual is 'called' has been emphasised by Christianity.* Martin Luther drew special attention to it; the sociologist Max Weber saw it as a defining feature of Western capitalism.

[169] Parel, Anthony J. (2006), *Gandhi's Philosophy and the Quest for Harmony*, Cambridge, Cambridge University Press, p. 5.

[170] *Mengzi (Mencius) in Sources of Chinese Tradition*, vol 1, pp. 147-54.

[171] Sources, p.164. Xunzi was an eclectic, primarily Confucian, thinker of the third century BCE.

172   *Aeschylus*, Agamemnon, 1327-30

173   *The prophet Teiresias in Euripides*, Bacchae 275-80.

174   *Journey to the West* by Wu Cheng'en, a Chinese folk tale based on a true story about a Buddhist monk, retold by Timothy Richard (Tokyo: Tuttle Publishiing, 2008), p. 100.

175   Marcus Aurelius, Meditations 5:24.

176   Marcus Aurelius Meditations 5: 21. *We find the same in Plato and in the Muslim philosopher-sociologist Ibn Khaldun* (d. 1406).

177   As the Greek philosopher Heraclitus (c. 500 BCE) put it.

178   Mithen, Steven, *The Prehistory of the Mind: a search for the origins of art, religion and science* (London: Thames and Hudson, 1996).

179   Mengzi in *Sources*, p. 155.

180   Xunzi (Hsun-Tzu) in Sources, pp. 161, 163

181   Silk, *Infinite Cosmos,* pp. 198-200, 210-12.

Index

About the author

Professor Antony Black was born in Leeds in 1936. He studied History and received his doctorate at the University of Cambridge. He lectured at the University of Dundee in the Department of Political Science and has been visiting professor at the University of Trento, the University of California (Riverside) and the National University of Singapore. He has lectured on Western political thought from Plato to the present day, Marxism, Islam, communitarianism and international relations.

His research has been on medieval political thought, theories of community, Islamic political thought from Muhammad to today, the differences between Islamic and Western political thought, and the political thought of ancient civilizations, including the Greeks, Mesopotamia to China.

Now he is working on ideas of the good life and how (if at all) this can be promoted by society and the state. How can we learn from both Western and Eastern thought, especially Confucianism? He is co-authoring a textbook on comparative and non-Western political thought.

He was brought up a Christian, became a Roman Catholic at Cambridge and at the age of fifty ceased to be a religious believer. He has been married twice and has five children.

Printed in Great Britain
by Amazon.co.uk, Ltd.,
Marston Gate.